SHORT WALKS FROM
——PUBS IN——
The Thames Valley

D1392096

SHORT WALKS FROM
—————— PUBS IN ——
The Thames Valley

Alan Charles

COUNTRYSIDE BOOKS
NEWBURY, BERKSHIRE

First Published 1995
© Alan Charles 1995

COUNTRYSIDE BOOKS
3 Catherine Road
Newbury, Berkshire

ISBN 1 85306 322 3

Designed by Mon Mohan
Cover illustration by Colin Doggett
Photographs by the author

Produced through MRM Associates Ltd., Reading
Typeset by The Midlands Book Typesetting Company, Loughborough
Printed by Woolnough Bookbinding Ltd., Irthlingborough

Contents

Publisher's Note

We hope that you obtain considerable enjoyment from this book; great care has been taken in its preparation. However, changes of landlord and actual closures are sadly not uncommon. Likewise, although at the time of publication all routes followed public rights of way or permitted paths, diversion orders can be made and permissions withdrawn.

We cannot of course be held responsible for such diversion orders and any inaccuracies in the text which result from these or any other changes to the routes nor any damage which might result from walkers trespassing on private property. We are anxious that all details covering the walks and the pubs are kept up to date and would therefore welcome information from readers which would be relevant to future editions.

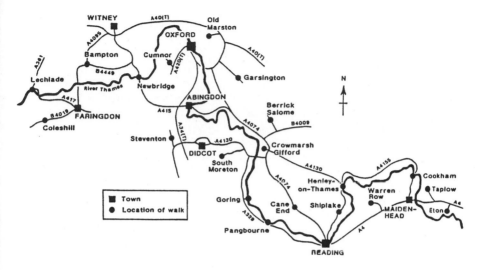

Area map showing locations of the walks.

Map Symbols

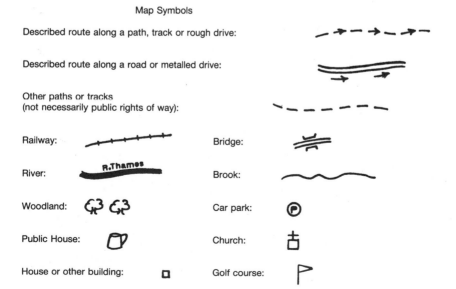

Described route along a path, track or rough drive:

Described route along a road or metalled drive:

Other paths or tracks
(not necessarily public rights of way):

Railway:

Bridge:

River: R.Thames

Brook:

Woodland:

Car park:

Public House:

Church:

House or other building:

Golf course:

Introduction

Whereas the ancient land routes across southern England – the Icknield Way, The Ridgeway, the Harrow Way and the Pilgrims' Way – were largely born of the landscape, the equally important river highway, the Thames, has to a great extent given birth to its landscape. Through time immemorial, the sinuous waverings of the river have levelled the land and, were it not for the hill-slopes beyond its borders, 'Thames Valley' would have seemed an inappropriate name for the countryside through which the river flows. It is among these hills and along this valley that some of England's most delightful towns and villages can be found; and it is in these towns and villages that the pubs featured in this book are situated.

The pubs have been carefully chosen – with comfort, atmosphere, cleanliness, quality and range of food and drink always in mind. Inns where food is highly-priced have been avoided, as have those where on Sundays there is either no food or only a roast lunch, this being the most popular day for walking. All of the pubs welcome families inside – not just in the garden. While some have a special menu for children, others offer them smaller portions at reduced prices. Most of the pubs have their own car parks and most landlords are happy for customers to leave their cars there while on the walk, if they are asked first.

The walks are chosen for their brevity (none is more than 3½ miles in length), ease of navigation and attractiveness. In total they draw from what is best along this landscape of the Thames – beautiful riverside paths and meadows, wide sweeping views of the valley, fine old towns and villages.

The walks can be traced on the well-known Landranger series of Ordnance Survey (OS) maps, which are on a scale of 1¼ inches to the mile. Ten of the walks can be followed on Landranger 175, seven on 164, two on 163 and one on 174. These maps are valuable to the walker since they show public rights of way in good detail. Also valuable are the OS/Philip's series of county street atlases. They are on a scale of 2½ inches to the mile and give the names of streets, farms, houses and pubs in addition to showing footpaths and bridleways, mostly very precisely placed, although their status as rights of way (or otherwise) is not given. Since no less than 16 of the walks are covered by the volume for Oxfordshire (available as a pocket edition), this may be a worthwhile investment.

Those familiar with grid reference numbers can use the OS maps and atlases to locate the exact position of each pub. The numbers are six figures in length and appear after details of the length of each walk.

Compass bearings are given throughout the text where these are thought to aid navigation. While stiles, gates, hedgerows, woodland, and so on are subject to the will of man, bearings are beyond his jurisdiction and remain (as far as makes no difference) just where they are!

Although I have avoided potentially difficult paths, I cannot entirely guarantee the absence of two of a walker's natural enemies – mud and nettles. And with some of the routes following short stretches of the Thames or other rivers it is inevitable that, after heavy or prolonged rain, progress along the riverside paths and meadows can become a foot-wetting experience. So to ensure that your day is as enjoyable as possible at such times, I strongly recommend the use of wellingtons – and, perhaps, a walking-stick to aid stability!

Happy walking!

Alan Charles
Spring 1995

1 Eton
The Hogshead

Previously known as the George, the Hogshead is situated at the southern end of Eton's High Street. Close by is Telford's Thames bridge, built in 1823 and closed to wheeled traffic since 1970. The Hogshead is one of a chain of traditional-style pubs offering a very wide range of cask ales. The enthusiast will take delight in the long line of polished handpumps on the bar, where up to 14 real ales are dispensed at any one time. Half of these are changed regularly and might include such oddities as Chocolate Fuggles! The draught Strongbow cider and the Heineken and Stella lagers seem to pale in comparison to all this!

The food menu boasts 'good ol' home cooking' and offers starters, main dishes, fish, sausages, salads, jacket potatoes and desserts. The main dishes include pies made on the premises, and the sausages are chosen from the range of 67 O'Hagen varieties (don't be surprised to find champagne and truffle sausages on offer!). Food is served every day from 12 noon to 2.30 pm (2 pm on Sunday) and 6 pm to 8.30 pm, except on Sunday evening. The opening hours are 11 am to 11 pm from Monday to Saturday, and 12 noon to 3 pm and 7 pm to 10.30 pm on Sunday. Accompanied children are very welcome inside during mealtimes. Dogs may only be taken into the patio garden.

Telephone: 01753 861797.

How to get there: The pub is in Eton High Street, a short distance north of the pedestrianised Thames bridge that links Eton to Windsor. There is a frequent train service every day from London (Paddington) to Windsor and Eton Central station, and from London (Waterloo) to Windsor and Eton Riverside station. Each station is a short walking distance from the pub.

Parking: The pub does not have its own car park, and roadside parking is limited. There are two small car parks nearby, but you are likely to find them full. The best advice is to leave your car at the Alma Road long-stay car park adjoining Alexandra Gardens, south of the river. The access to this can be found from the junction of the A332 with the A308, by going along the road signposted to Windsor town centre. Having parked, it's a simple matter of walking through the gardens and alongside the river (with the river on your left) to the bridge and crossing this to the pub.

Length of the walk: 3¼ miles. Map: OS Landranger 175 Reading, Windsor and surrounding area or 176 West London area (inn GR 967773).

The walk crosses the Thames bridge and follows the river past Romney Lock to Home Park – where there's an excellent view of Windsor Castle. After re-crossing the river to Datchet's golf course, it enters the outer precincts of Eton College and continues along the entire length of Eton's historic High Street.

11

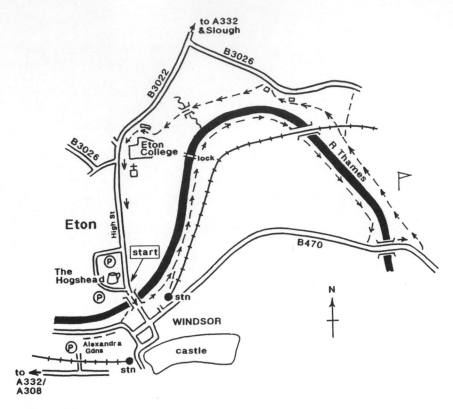

The Walk

Cross the pedestrianised Thames bridge (to the castle side) and descend the 'Thames Side' steps on the left. After passing the Donkey House pub join a fenced tarmac path (Romney Walk) alongside the river. Riverside station and Windsor Castle will be in view on your right. The path runs into a tarmac drive, which takes you forward between the river and the railway. A pumping station and cottage inscribed with 'VRI 1898' is the next feature, followed by a boatyard. Romney Lock, which is beyond a footbridge on the left, was built in 1797 in order to control the winter floods. Cross the boatyard to a stile and go straight on in a riverside meadow. Passing under a railway arch (a branch line to Windsor) continue forward along the water's edge – and enjoy one of the best views of Windsor Castle!

The next objective is to cross the river by the Victoria Bridge ahead, but in order to do this you will need to walk away from the river across the grass (unless you have spotted a quicker way!). Notice two plaques on the bridge as you go over. One relates to its construction in 1851, the other to its reconstruction in 1966. Having arrived on the opposite side, continue along the pavement for 120 yards and turn left onto a

Eton College and chapel.

gravel track. This crosses a golf course and marks the turning point of the walk. After the track fades away you will need to continue on the grass to the far end of the golf course and make your exit through a gap in the corner.

A little beyond the gap a signpost has two fingers pointing under the railway (that Windsor branch again). Take the left-hand option and go under a low arch (keep your head down!), then through a gate and straight on over a meadow, crossing a concrete bridge en route. From the far end of the meadow a pair of stiles will transfer you across a rough drive to a path opposite. This in its turn takes you to the left of Eton College boathouse and across its slipway to a road, the B3026. Go forward on the road and join a path on the left beyond Boathouse Cottage. A footbridge will lead you into the Eton College playing fields along a well-laid path. The college buildings come into view ahead while a brick bridge takes you forward over a branch of the Thames.

Turn right when you reach the college forecourt (not before), and left under a stone arch, then pass between college buildings to Eton's High Street. Turn left and walk the length of the High Street, with the college chapel at the start and numerous college buildings and interesting shops thereafter – including the delightful Asquith's Teddy Bear Shop.

You will find the pub at the far end of the High Street, near the river bridge.

2 Taplow
The Oak and Saw

There could hardly be a more pleasing situation for a public house – overlooking the village green and accompanied by delightful cottage terraces and the parish church. In a pub 'formerly frequented by woodcutters', all comers (including families) enjoy a warm welcome. You can choose a good meal from the 'Quick Bite' or 'Main Menu' board. The snacks include a variety of sandwiches, baguettes and ploughman's lunches. Examples from the main menu are Hungarian goulash, gammon steak, home-made lasagne and (for which the Oak and Saw is famous) good old bangers and mash! Beef burritos require a sentence to themselves – 'spicy parcels on a bed of salsa, with sour cream, salad and fries'. The Oak and Saw omelette is no less creative, being made with onions, peppers, tomatoes and cheese. Meals are served from 12 noon to 2.30 pm and 6.30 pm to 9.30 pm on Monday to Saturday, and from 12 noon to 2 pm and 7 pm to 9.30 pm on Sunday, with a full menu throughout.

Up to six real ales are on offer at any one time, and there are three draught lagers – Foster's, Kronenbourg and Budweiser. There are also some good quality house wines. Draught cider is Blackthorn Dry. The opening hours are 12 noon to 3 pm and 5.30 pm to 11 pm from Monday to Thursday, 12 noon to 11 pm on Friday and Saturday, and 12 noon to 3 pm and 7 pm to 10.30 pm on Sunday. Well-behaved dogs are welcome in the bar or in the garden.

Telephone: 01628 604074.

How to get there: The Oak and Saw lies close to the B3026, a mile west of Burnham. If coming from the south, join the B3026 (Taplow Road) from the A4 roundabout near Sainsbury's supermarket and stay with this when it becomes Boundary Road. The pub can be located by turning off this road into Taplow's High Street or into the road signposted 'Taplow'. With the pub being close to the parish church, your best point of reference is the tall green spire!

Parking: In the pub's car park or in the clearly signposted public car park beside the parish hall.

Length of the walk: 3½ miles. Map: OS Landranger 175 Reading, Windsor and surrounding area (inn GR 912822).

An excellent walk along bridlepaths and country lanes, with views of Windsor Castle and the Thames Valley. Hitcham's attractive parish church and Hitcham Farmhouse are met at the halfway point and Taplow Vineyard near the end.

Good footwear is strongly advised for this walk, and wellingtons would not be out of place in winter or during wet weather.

The Walk
Turn right on leaving the Oak and Saw and right again into a footpath by the telephone box opposite St Nicolas' church. The path runs between hedges and terminates at a kissing gate, giving access to a field. Turn left and follow the field edge to another kissing gate in the far left-hand corner. Cross the road there to a footpath almost opposite, then continue in the same direction as previously along a narrow path, with a hedge and trees on the left. Looking across the meadow to the right you will have one of the best views of Windsor Castle – in line with the road just crossed and at a distance of 5 miles. At the far end of the path turn left

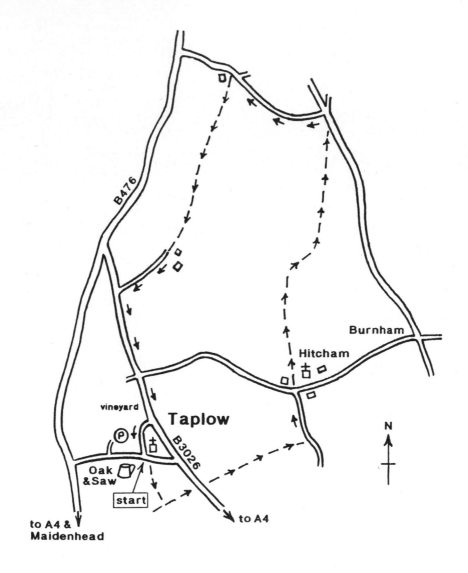

B476

Burnham

Hitcham

vineyard

Taplow

P

Oak
&Saw

start

B3026

to A4 &
Maidenhead

to A4

N

Church cottages, Taplow.

into a road and follow this up to Hitcham Lane at a T-junction.

Before crossing Hitcham Lane to a bridleway opposite, why not walk a few yards along the road to the right? You will find St Mary's church, with its attractive Tudor brick tower, and beyond that the massive timber-framed Hitcham Farmhouse, with brick nogging and a superb tiled roof.

Now back to that bridleway (by Cloverdown House), which will take you between paddocks to the left and a hedge to the right. The land beyond the hedge is that of Hitcham Park, whose gate piers can be seen on the far side. These, along with a tall garden wall (which you may not so easily see), is all that survives of Hitcham Manor House.

The bridleway eventually bears right while running uphill to a wood, where there are numerous sweet chestnut trees. It reverts to its previous direction, but now as a wide track through the wood. You should ignore a waymark post halfway along the wooded stretch and stay with the track to a road and T-junction. Turn left there into Huntswood Lane. With the wood now on your left, go along the road for ¼ mile to Paddock Bungalow, the first house on the left. Turn left into the bridleway prior to the bungalow and follow this just inside the wood for ½ mile, until it runs into a road by Hitchambury Manor.

Keep forward on the road (Hunts Lane) to its T-junction with the B3026 and there turn left. After ¼ mile go over the crossing by the lovely old Church Cottages (boldly inscribed '1853') and soon arrive at the entrance to Taplow Vineyard – a worthwhile diversion for the good English wine that is available. It is open for free tasting and for sale of wine from 8 am to 12.30 pm and 1.30 pm to 5 pm from Monday to Thursday.

Back on the B3026, pass another fine cottage terrace and soon turn right into Taplow's High Street, following this down to the Oak and Saw.

3 Cookham
The Royal Exchange

The Old Butcher's Shop, Ovey's Farm, The Old Apothecary – a village then and a village still, busy with summer visitors and local traffic but retaining much of its old world charm. As a building the Royal Exchange has been part of this scene for more than 500 years. The fact that it functioned as a centre for money-lending explains the name 'Coin Exchange', with which it was christened when first becoming a licensed house. A feature attracting much interest is its hallway, which was once a duelling alley. Whether this was connected in any way with money-lending, I'm not sure!

The regular menu includes a good choice of starters and main dishes. There is lasagne verdi, Cajun chicken and hot 'n' spicy chicken. Exotic balti dishes 'from the roof of the world' are based on chicken, lamb or vegetables. There are steaks in various permutations and dishes served in 'sizzling skillets'. Those with a less demanding appetite can opt for ploughman's lunches, sandwiches, macaroni cheese and other traditional fare. Daily specials expand the choice further, and include vegetarian dishes. Meals are served from 12 noon to 2 pm and 6 pm to 9.30 pm on Monday to Saturday, and 12 noon to 3 pm and 7 pm to 9.30 pm on Sunday. The same menu applies throughout, except that on Sundays no sandwiches are available. Reservations are normally advised for the popular Sunday roast lunch.

There are four real ales (three plus a guest), two very nice draught ciders (Addlestones and Olde English) and four draught lagers. The pub is open 'all day' from Monday to Saturday (11 am to 11 pm), and 12 noon to 3 pm and 7 pm to 10.30 pm on Sunday. Families are welcome and can be accommodated in the lounge bar. If kept on a lead, well-behaved dogs may be taken inside or into the garden.

Telephone: 01628 520085.

How to get there: Cookham lies on the south bank of the Thames, 3 miles north of Maidenhead. The pub is along the High Street, the A4094. Cookham railway station is about a mile from the pub. In general there is an hourly service from London (Paddington) every day, but there are no trains on Sundays from October to March inclusive. For Cookham go downhill from the station.

Parking: In the pub's small car park. Alternatively, in the National Trust car park 300 yards west of the High Street along the Cookham Dean road.

Length of the walk: 3¼ miles. Map: OS Explorer 3 Chiltern Hills South or Landranger 175 Reading, Windsor and surrounding area (inn GR 897855).

After following a lovely stretch of the Thames the path turns inland across Cockmarsh, a Site of Special Scientific Interest owned by the National Trust. The return route is along a level path below the hills and provides superb views across the Thames Valley to the Chilterns.

The Walk
On leaving the Royal Exchange go left to the High Street and left again at the road junction. Note the Tarry Stone on the opposite pavement 'at which sports were held before AD 1507' and soon turn left into a no through road, signposted to the church. Take the left-hand of the two paths through the churchyard, and, passing to the left of the church, shortly find yourself on the bank of the river Thames. Turn left there and follow the river, soon through two gates and forward for ½ mile along riverside meadows to a third gate. This gives entry to Cockmarsh, 132 acres of grazing land owned by the National Trust, a Site of Special Scientific Interest on account of its 'unusual plant, insect and bird life'.

Walk forward between a line of trees and the river bank, and continue under a railway bridge. As well as the branch railway line to Bourne End and Marlow, the bridge carries the Thames Path to the opposite bank.

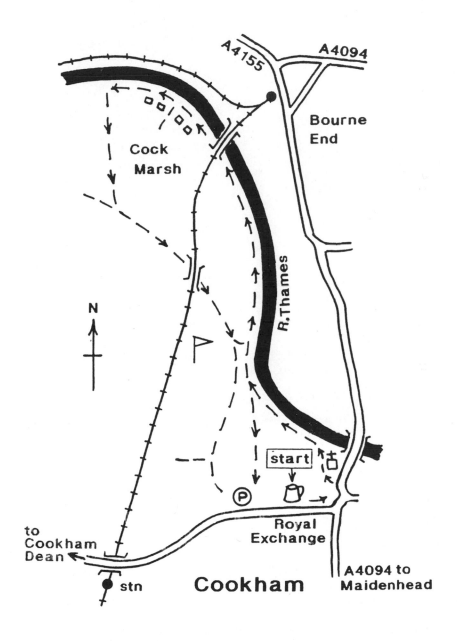

A4155 A4094

Bourne
End

Cock
Marsh

R.Thames

N

start

to
Cookham
Dean

P

Royal
Exchange

stn

A4094 to
Maidenhead

Cookham

The Thames near Cookham.

This path traces the river for 175 miles from its source to the Thames Barrier – a walk you could keep for another day!

After passing a number of summer houses and the Bounty Riverside Inn, you will rejoin Cockmarsh, where a further stretch along the river bank will take you to a gate. Don't go through the gate (which leads into a cultivated field) but turn left, leaving the river behind and following a shallow ditch and trees on the right. The prominent mound in the meadow over to your left is a Bronze Age burial site. When the ditch and trees go off to the right, continue forward and cross a low footbridge to a terraced path below the hillside. Turn left onto this wide path and, with a view of the Chiltern Hills beyond the Thames Valley, eventually cross a stile and follow a line of hornbeam trees.

Go under a railway arch and over a stile (not through the adjacent gate), then forward on a level path. The right of way is now along the edge of a golf course, but a more pleasant 'permissive' path runs parallel on the left between a ditch and a hedge. On arrival at a three-way signpost you can either turn left and rejoin the Thames or continue with the ditch along a less exposed route to the National Trust car park. For the river option turn left over a concrete footbridge and head straight for the river. Once there turn right and follow the river for just 75 yards to where – by a tall black poplar tree – it starts to curve left.

For the car park leave the river by keeping straight on across the grass to the right-hand of two distant gates (190°). For the High Street and the pub you could aim for the left-hand of the two gates (180° – nearer the houses and to the right of a wooden shed) or simply stay with the river and make your return via the churchyard.

Places of interest nearby
If time is on your side you could follow the walk with a visit to the *Spencer Art Gallery* in the High Street. Sir Stanley Spencer was born in Cookham in 1891 in a house almost opposite the Royal Exchange.

4 Warren Row
The Crooked Inn

Set in a quiet village 2 miles south of the Thames, the Crooked Inn has in the past owned two other names – the Frog and Toad and the Old House at Home. With its attractive proportions this red-brick, tile-hung pub is anything but crooked!

The regular menu includes starters, a wide range of ploughman's lunches and filled jacket potatoes, home-made pie of the day, Chef's Amazing Curry and Crooked Inn Brunch. The specials menu is changed every few days and could include such delectable dishes as roast duck breast with glazed pineapple and black pepper sauce or sauté of pork fillet with honey and apple. Further good-value options are the Monday to Friday business lunches (not restricted to business people!) and the Sunday roast. Food is available every day from 12 noon to 2 pm and 7 pm to 9.30 pm (9 pm on Sunday). The choice of items on the bar menu may be reduced somewhat at Sunday lunchtime, because of the popularity of the roast meal.

In addition to a guest ale, there are three regular real ales, Wadworth 6X, Courage Best and Brakspear Ordinary. Blackthorn Dry cider and Foster's and Kronenbourg lagers are on draught and there are four house wines by the glass. The wine list provides upwards of 20 wines. The pub is open from 11.30 am to 3 pm and 6 pm to 11 pm on Monday to Saturday, and 12 noon to 3 pm and 7 pm to 10.30 pm on Sunday. Families may take their offspring into the restaurant. The same doesn't apply to the garden, because there isn't one! Well-behaved dogs are allowed in the bar, but not in the restaurant.

Telephone: 01628 825861.

How to get there: Warren Row is signposted (1 mile) from the A4, some 3 miles west of Maidenhead at Knowl Hill. It is also signposted from the A4130, 1½ miles east of Henley at Remenham Hill (via Cockpole Green). The pub is in the main street and easily found.

Parking: In the pub's car park or along the roadside nearby.

Length of the walk: 2½ miles. Map: OS Landranger 175 Reading, Windsor and surrounding area (inn GR 812808).

A straightforward walk enjoying classic views of the Thames Valley against a backcloth of the Chiltern Hills. It passes below the slopes of Ashley Hill and enjoys easy-going tracks and field paths while circulating around Channers, a small Forestry Commission wood.

The Walk
Turn left on leaving the Crooked Inn and pass both the 'tin' chapel and a long terrace of houses, then turn left into a short drive between Queen

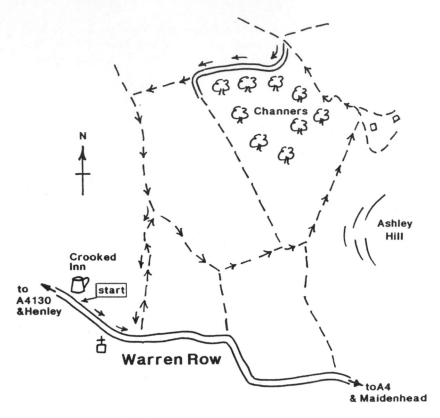

Anne Cottage and Hill View. A signpost on the opposite side of the road points the way. After passing garages, soon cross a stile and continue forward – between a fence and field to the left and trees to the right. The Thames Valley now comes into view ahead and Ashley Hill through the trees on the right.

The fence goes its own way when you arrive at another stile. Turn right into the bridleway here and follow this between fields (with trees on the left) to its meeting with a wide track, where stands a metal signpost. Turn left to a stile and gate and go uphill on the track between fields. Ignore a stile in the fence on the right and continue uphill until the track turns left. Go over a stile on the right at this point and keep going up – in the same direction as previously and not omitting to look back at the excellent view! Stay on the track as it turns half-left from a stile and goes in and out of a dip. When it terminates at a stile, continue forward alongside a wire fence to a stile at the far end. This is under an electricity pole and connects with another path at a T-junction.

After turning left here (there is a house in the other direction) you should soon ignore a three-way signpost and stile on the right – but not the view across the Thames Valley to the Chiltern Hills! Stay on the path as it skirts an area of scrub and goes into the straight alongside a wood. On arrival at a junction of ways beyond a corner of the wood, turn very sharp left into a concrete drive. The chalk pit in view, $1/4$ mile or so to your right, is part of a nature reserve owned and managed by the Berks, Bucks and Oxfordshire Naturalists Trust. Acquired by the Trust in 1964, it was their very first purchase. Follow the drive as it curves round between the wood edge and a field. When it eventually turns left keep straight on to a stile and gate. Go forward through one field to another and descend the hill straight on to a 'V' stile at the bottom.

After turning left into the hedge-lined bridleway at the bottom, you may notice that some walkers have used a parallel footpath higher up on the right – doubtless to avoid the mud! Follow the bridleway or footpath uphill for $1/4$ mile to the first stile (on the right if viewed from the bridleway), which you will recognise from earlier in the walk. It's now a matter of treading the first part of the walk in reverse. For this, cross the stile (or simply turn right if using the higher path) and walk briefly through the trees, then follow a fence until it eventually turns right in a field corner. Go over a stile there and soon join a drive leading to the road at Warren Row. Turn right into the road for the Crooked Inn.

5 Henley-on-Thames
The Anchor

For many, Henley-on-Thames needs no introduction. It is well known for its Royal Regatta, its marvellous river-scape, its many fine buildings and, to the real ale enthusiast, its Brakspear Brewery. The Anchor is a Brakspear pub, one of many in the town, and dates back to the 17th century.

You can choose from a very extensive menu on any day from 12 noon to 2 pm and 7 pm to 9 pm (9.30 pm on Sunday). It includes seafood, pasta and vegetarian meals and 'old country-style' food – home-made pies and the like. In addition there are salads, sandwiches, filled jacket potatoes and a variety of international dishes, also a goodly choice of desserts. 'Kids' Corner' is a menu designed especially for children.

Opening hours from Monday to Saturday are 11 am to 11 pm during the summer (approximately March to October), and 11 am to 3 pm and 5 pm to 11 pm during the winter. Sunday opening is from 12 noon to 3 pm and 7 pm to 10.30 pm throughout the year. You can enjoy Brakspear real ale, Scrumpy Jack cider, a popular South African wine, Heineken or Stella lagers or one of a wide selection of malt whiskies. You could also have one of three varieties of coffee. A warm welcome is offered to well-behaved children. Dogs, however, are not really permitted inside – partly on account of Cognac, the pub's resident hound. There is a large patio garden at the rear of the pub. Accommodation is available in two rooms.

Telephone: 01491 574753.

How to get there: The Anchor is in Friday Street, close to the west bank of the Thames and south of the Thames bridge. Trains from London (Paddington) via Twyford run hourly every day (no service on Sundays from October to March inclusive). On leaving the station turn right by the Imperial Hotel and follow the road round to the left. Friday Street will then be on your left.

Parking: In the pub's own small car park or in a pay and display area. One of these is near the town hall and has a three hour limit. There is a long-stay car park adjacent to the Thames, 1/4 mile south of Friday Street. Access is along Meadow Road.

Length of the walk: 3 miles. Map: OS Landranger 175 Reading, Windsor and surrounding area or Explorer 3 Chiltern Hills South (inn GR 763825).

After crossing the 18th-century bridge the walk follows one of the most beautiful stretches of the river Thames – the Henley Reach. It enjoys an unparalleled view of Temple Island and Wren's Fawley Court before turning 'inland' through the delightful precincts of Remenham village.

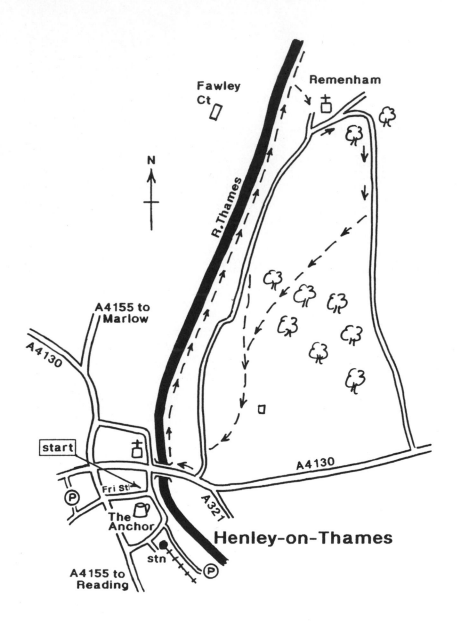

Fawley
Ct

Remenham

R.Thames

N

A4155 to
Marlow

A4130

start

A4130

Fri St

A321

The
Anchor

A4155 to
Reading

stn

Henley-on-Thames

The Brewery at Henley.

Beyond Remenham a short hill places the walk on an elevated field – where views of the Thames Valley must be seen to be believed!

The Walk

On leaving the Anchor turn left out of Friday Street and make a bee line for the Thames bridge. Having crossed the bridge and been confronted by a bouquet of road signs, turn left into one of two signposted footpaths – the one that passes to the right of a house called 'Tollgate'. You will soon be on the riverside path and enjoying a view of the opposite bank – including the famous Henley Brewery, which has been here since 1779. If the time and wind is right, you will enjoy its aromas for the entirety of the walk!

Fawley Court also comes into view, but not until you have walked a mile of footpath – the 'straight mile' of the Henley Royal Regatta which is held annually in the first week of July. Fawley Court was designed by Wren and built in 1684, and the grounds laid out by 'Capability' Brown almost a century later. What better credentials could you have for what is now a Marian Fathers Retreat Centre! Temple Island can be seen $^{1}/_{2}$ mile further down river. The temple itself was built in 1771 merely to enhance the view from Fawley Court.

Unless you wish to obtain a closer view of the temple you should turn right to a stile after crossing a cattle grid. There is a signpost pointing

31

that way. Having crossed the stile go along a wide track between high walls and soon find yourself beside St Nicholas' church, Remenham. Turn left at the road junction beyond the church and branch right into Remenham Church Lane opposite the Old School House. As you ascend the hill your view Thamesward includes Greenlands, 'a sumptuous 19th century Italianate mansion' once owned by W. H. Smith the stationer. The lane curves right under trees and then runs almost straight and level between hedges. After walking 250 yards of this straightness you should go through a gap on the right – just before a single venerable oak tree.

Cross the very large field here half-right (230°) towards the right-hand extremity of the main body of a distant wood. Passing close to an electricity pole enter the wood and follow the main path uphill through the trees. Leave the wood from a stile beyond the summit and keep straight on across the grass, meeting a path coming in from the right, rear, at a three-way signpost. Continuing forward along the boundary between trees and a sloping meadow, soon pass under the trees to a stile. From the stile cross a large, well-kept lawn to its far end and continue forward again to the far left-hand corner of a meadow. A gate will place you on a road where you should turn left. Follow the road round to the right and soon join the A4130 by the Little Angel pub. Finally cross the river bridge and turn left for the Anchor.

6 Shiplake
The Plowden Arms

As an alehouse the Plowden Arms can trace its history back to 1749. Known as the Plough for more than 150 years it took on the present name in the 1930s, confirming its connection with the Plowden family of nearby Shiplake Court. Diversification was not unusual in public houses of an earlier day. Here at the Plough (as it then was) an undertaker made coffins while his subjects were kept in the cellar – along with the beer! Today the pub is a model of comfort and sociability, and a warm welcome is offered to everyone.

Food choices are all on the blackboard and include a variety of dishes made on the premises – steak and onion pie, crunchy-topped cauliflower cheese, beef in Brakspear ale, for example. Fish figures prominently and there are some excellent curries. Sandwiches are made with fresh bread (that's why they are not available on Sundays). The home-made desserts are enough to keep you from the walk a little longer, especially when it's Norfolk treacle tart or rich chocolate cheesecake. Meals are available every day from 12 noon to 2 pm and from 7 pm to 9.30 pm, with the exception of Monday and Sunday evenings. Apart from the sandwiches, a full menu is available throughout.

In addition to a guest ale, Brakspear real ales are on draught, as well as Strongbow cider, Heineken and Stella lagers and Guinness. Opening hours are from 11.30 am to 2.30 pm and 6 pm to 11 pm on Monday to Saturday, and 12 noon to 3 pm and 7 pm to 10.30 pm on Sunday. Children may be taken into the family room, where they can run around to their hearts' content! Dogs are welcome, but in the garden only.

Telephone: 01734 402794.

How to get there: The pub is easily found – on the A4155, midway between Reading and Henley-on-Thames. You must ignore any road signs that might tempt you off the A4155!

Parking: In the pub's own car park or nearby along the road signposted to Binfield Heath and Peppard. Please consult the landlord if you wish to leave your car in the pub car park while you are on the walk.

Length of the walk: 3 miles. Map: OS Landranger 175 Reading, Windsor and surrounding area (inn GR 765784).

You will find part of this walk so 'out of this world' that I am certain that you will be happy to tread it twice over – on the way out and on the way back. This is where the Thames curves around the watery levels of Borough Marsh and flows past Phillimore's Island to Shiplake Lock. The circular part of the walk, albeit short, enjoys views of Wargrave and the Thames that are second to none.

The Walk

From the Plowden Arms cross the main road (the A4155) to Church Lane, a no through road. You will find the parish church at the end of

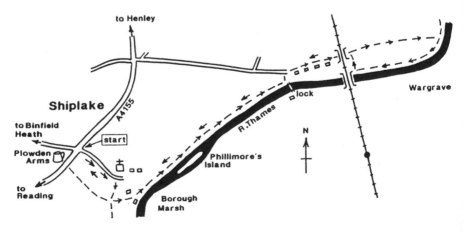

The river Thames and Wargrave Manor.

the lane – in its marvellous situation overlooking the Thames. It was in this church that the poet Alfred Lord Tennyson married Emily Sellwood in 1850. The church's other claim to fame is by virtue of its medieval stained glass. This glass came from a ruined abbey in France and had been buried for safe-keeping during the French Revolution.

From the triangular parking area by the church bear right and go downhill on an uneven path. Where a part-tarmac drive comes in from the right turn left onto a track and soon find yourself at the green by Shiplake College boathouse. Go forward across the green to the waterside (not on the uphill drive) and walk between the trees and the river – an idyllic place to be sure! Passing in sight of Phillimore's Island and the watery meadows beyond the opposite shore, stay with the river all the way to Shiplake Lock (3/4 mile from the boathouse). For viewing the lock turn right over a footbridge, but to continue on the walk turn left onto a metalled path alongside a flint wall. The path will soon place you at a road end, where this changes to a rough drive.

Turn right into the drive, and, walking between the houses and the fields, eventually pass under a railway arch – the branch line from Twyford to Henley. Cross a stile here and go straight on in a meadow, with a wire fence on your left and accompanied (perhaps) by flocks of Canada geese, a common sight in these parts. Wargrave directly ahead looks very fine, as does Wargrave Manor on the hilltop. On arrival at the far end of the meadow, go over a stile and turn right. There are steps here leading down to a small landing stage – a ferry embarkation point, sadly no longer in use. Follow the river, with a fence and the meadow on the right, all the way to the railway, at the place where it crosses the river. Go over a stile here (on the right) and re-enter the meadow, walking alongside the railway to a stile in the next corner.

If you haven't already twigged, this is 'where you came in', and you now have the pleasant task of retracing your steps back to the pub. To do this, go back under the railway and turn left into a short path beyond the last house, then turn right over a stile and follow the river bank back to Shiplake College boathouse. Passing to the right of the boathouse, go forward on a track and turn right at a crossing, where an uphill path will take you back to the church. Church Lane is now all that comes between you and the Plowden Arms.

7 Cane End
The Fox

The Fox is an impressively large Brewers Fayre pub in a commanding position beside the Reading to Wallingford road. Inside, you will immediately feel at home in a beautifully furbished open-plan area.

The appetising food includes savoury dishes, hot platters, fresh salads, light bites and sandwiches. These are backed up with a selection of daily specials and desserts and no less than eight varieties of speciality coffees. Children have their own colourful Charlie Chalk menu card, which offers a good choice of main courses – all with vegetables and potato alphabet letters. Meals are available every day between 11.30 am (12 noon on Sunday) and 10 pm. The regular menus apply throughout these times. There are usually three real ales, examples being Gale's Best, HSB and 5X, as well as Heineken and Stella lagers, Scrumpy Jack cider and a wide choice of wines by the glass. The bar is open 'all day' (11 am to 11 pm) on Monday to Saturday, and from 12 noon to 3 pm and 7 pm to 10.30 pm on Sunday.

Children are highly thought-of, and can enjoy the Charlie Chalk Play Zone, a separate room for letting off steam, while remaining under your watchful eye. Special play equipment will keep them fully occupied outside, too. Dogs are welcome, but in the garden only.

Telephone: 01734 723116.

How to get there: The Fox is easily found – on the A4074, 5 miles north-west of Reading.

Parking: In the pub's large car park. Alternatively, you could leave your car in a quiet lane nearby. For this, go along Horsepond Road adjacent to the Fox (signposted to Kidmore End) and turn first left.

Length of the walk: 2¼ miles. Map: OS Landranger 175 Reading, Windsor and surrounding area (inn GR 679795).

An attractive walk running uphill and down dale (but not too steeply) through woodland and across fields. It visits the little hamlet of Nuney Green and passes the fruit farm at Cross Lanes.

The Walk

From the Fox cross the main road (the A4074) to a gate and stile near the S-bend sign, then go through a thinly planted copse to another gate and stile. Bear right across a short stretch of grass to a metal pedestrian gate and from there take the straight path between a field to the left and a paddock to the right, aiming for the left-hand end of the woodland ahead. Red-brick Cane End House is in view over to your right as you walk this path.

Passing through a gap at the end of the straight path turn right into a field corner and enter the wood. A wide track will soon take you forward through the wood and back into the open – with a field to the left and the wood to the right. When the track re-enters the wood ignore a right-hand branch and keep straight on (along with the white arrows) and slightly uphill. When it comes to within a few yards of a field on the right ignore a stile on the right and take the clear left-branching path back into the wood (250°). A bungalow comes into view and you are soon at a crossing in the peaceful hamlet of Nuney Green.

Turn left so that the bungalow (Cross Ways) is on your right, and go straight on along a track ignoring a footpath on the right very soon. After passing a tennis court and the magnificent thatched Nuneywood Cottage (where the track evolves into a path), keep straight on under the trees. Stay with the path as it runs into a dip, turns left and ascends the hill to a bungalow and a road. Turn left into the road and walk as far as the road junction by Cross Lanes Fruit Farm and shop. If you have timed it right (Wednesday to Sunday from late August to Christmas) you could come away with some of the 20 varieties of apples, plums and pears!

So, perhaps with apple in hand, turn left onto a path immediately beyond the farm. This is signposted 'Cane End ¾' and takes you alongside the orchards and eventually into a dip. Ignore the path running away to the left along the dip and go over a stile leading

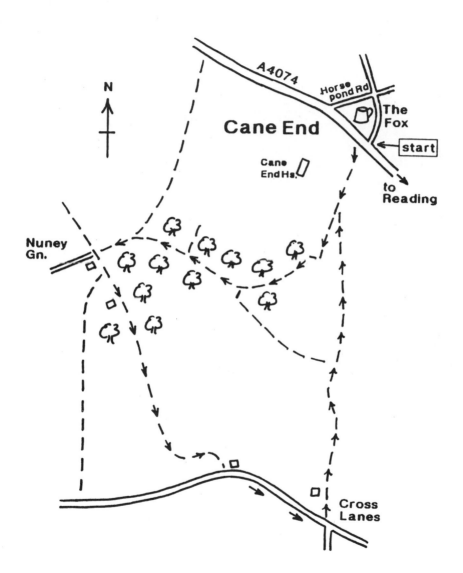

N

A4074

Horse pond Rd

Cane End

The Fox

start

Cane End Hs.

to Reading

Nuney Gn.

Cross Lanes

into a field. Climb the field straight on towards a clump of tall trees at the top (360°). Having crossed a stile up there, you should make your way more or less straight on through a planting of young trees and cross a level field to a metal gate – the gate met with at the start of the walk. Bearing left from the gate you will soon be back at the A4074 opposite the Fox.

8 Pangbourne
The Swan

A modelling enthusiast would find this lively, compact town an ideal subject. What more could he want? There are railway bridges and a station, a lock and weir, shops, pubs, a toll bridge over the Thames, the river Pang flowing in. The illustrations for Kenneth Grahame's *Wind in the Willows* were based on this stretch of the Thames and the journeyings of Jerome K. Jerome's *Three Men in a Boat* ended here. So Ratty and Mole and those three intrepid boatmen could well figure in the layout!

In the real world, the Swan overlooks the Thames and its weir in a situation which explains much of the popularity of the pub. Inside, the Swan is loosely divided into comfortable dining areas, giving a sense of seclusion wherever you sit. The conservatory provides a marvellous view of the river. This is an Artist's Fare pub and offers the regular menu that is found in all of its branches. This includes starters, salads and ploughman's lunches, a wide range of appetising main courses, vegetarian dishes and desserts. There is also a colourful children's menu. The Swan has, in addition, its own bar snacks and 'specials' menus. All the food is available every day from 12 noon to 10 pm, with the exception of Sunday when the bar snack menu is not provided – which results in only a marginal reduction in the choice.

The real ales are Morland Original and Old Speckled Hen and one other ale, which varies. Strongbow cider is on draught, as well as Foster's, Kronenbourg and Stella lagers. An extensive choice of wines is available by the glass or bottle. The bar is open from 11 am to 11 pm on Monday to Saturday, and from 12 noon to 3 pm and 7 pm to 10.30 pm on Sunday. Children may be taken into the conservatory or the small family area. Both are for non-smokers. Dogs are allowed, but in the patio garden only.

Telephone: 01734 844494.

How to get there: The Swan is easily found – on the A329 Wallingford to Reading road, near Pangbourne's railway station. There is a train service from London (Paddington) and Oxford twice-hourly from Monday to Saturday, hourly on Sunday.

Parking: In the pub's own small car park. Alternatively, you could leave your car in one of the pay and display car parks passed early in the walk. The first is on the A329 beyond the first railway bridge; the second is on the Pangbourne side of the Thames toll bridge (B471). If these are full try the unrestricted part of Horseshoe Road. This is linked to the Reading Road (A329) opposite the Star pub.

Length of the walk: 3 miles. Map: OS Landranger 175 Reading, Windsor and surrounding area (inn GR 633767).

Once clear of the shops and railway the walk joins the Thames towpath from the Pangbourne side of the old toll bridge. It crosses the National Trust's Pangbourne Meadow, from where there are superb views downriver against a backcloth of the Chiltern Hills. The route soon turns 'inland' across country, eventually meeting the highly acclaimed river Pang and following this back into Pangbourne.

The Walk

From the Swan go under the railway then left into the High Street opposite the Copper Inn. Turn left into Whitchurch Road (B471) by the George Hotel and follow this to a small car park on the right (where you may have left your car) just before the toll bridge. From inside the car park go through a barrier and soon join the grassy bank of the river. Turn right and follow the river through the National Trust's Pangbourne Meadow to a kissing gate at the far end. This 7-acre meadow was purchased by the Trust as far back as 1936. Go through a gate at the end of the next meadow and over a concrete footbridge to another gate, beyond which is a notice prohibiting mooring and bathing. Once through the second of this pair of gates leave the Thames by walking

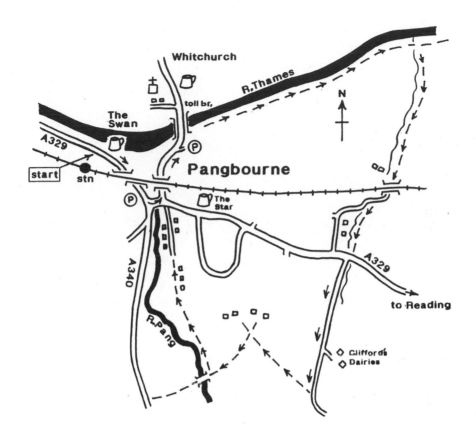

'inland' alongside a stream – which flows under that footbridge.

Pass through a field gap and follow closely the meanderings of the stream for ⅓ mile to a stile and a railway arch, ignoring all gates and branches en route. Go under the arch and turn right along a drive, following this for a short distance to a footpath signpost. Leave the drive here by turning left into a field and once again walking alongside the stream – the same one as previously. Cross the A329 road from the far end of the field and continue forward along a relatively quiet road between houses and the stream.

When the road turns left after ½ mile (not the drive to Clifford's Dairies) go over a stile on the right and enter a field. With houses in view ahead, cross this field to a stile and footbridge (310°), then keep straight on across a meadow (with two footbridges en route) to a gate and four-way signpost on the far side. Don't go through the gate but turn left and follow the hedge to a stile (there are allotments on the other side of the hedge). From the stile turn half-right (240°) across

43

Church cottages, Whitchurch.

another meadow towards, but not over, a footbridge – which may not be visible until you are close to it. The bridge crosses the Pang, a much respected trout stream.

Turn right so that the stream is on your left. Stay with it until it swings left, then keep straight on across the grass to a gate. Go forward from the gate along a narrow path behind gardens and in due course join a roughly surfaced drive between houses. The far end of the drive places you in the heart of Pangbourne opposite the George Hotel. For the Swan turn left into the High Street, then right to the A329 and go under the railway bridge.

Places of interest nearby
For a pleasant extension to the walk, cross the toll bridge to a short drive (a public right of way) on the left. Here you will find Church Cottages overlooking the mill and its pond in a most delightful situation.

Goring
The Miller of Mansfield

9

This historic village stands at the meeting point of three ancient highways – The Ridgeway, the Icknield Way and the river Thames – so it's not surprising that numerous artefacts have been unearthed here, representing life from Neolithic through to Saxon times. Nature and man have joined forces to make this one of the most beautiful and spectacular regions along the Thames Valley. The Miller of Mansfield plays a notable part in this, with its attractive proportions and situation, fully complemented inside by its atmosphere and cosiness.

The menu offers a choice of sandwiches, baguettes, ploughman's lunches and jacket potatoes. There is also a variety of main meals, of which steak and mushroom pie, barbecue rack of ribs and fillet of plaice are typical examples. When presented with their own colourful menu, children will feel that they are highly regarded. Fish becomes 'Devils', ham becomes 'Dinosaur', ice-cream with chocolate sauce becomes 'Polar Bear' and orange juice becomes 'Ice Fire'! A full menu is offered from 12 noon to 2.30 pm and 6 pm to 10 pm every day.

The real ales include Wadworth 6X, Courage Best and Ruddles County. Dry Blackthorn cider and Kronenbourg, Budweiser and Foster's lagers are on draught. Opening times are from 11 am to 11 pm on

45

Monday to Saturday, and from 12 noon to 3 pm and 7 pm to 10.30 pm
on Sunday. Your dog may be brought inside, if kept on a lead. There is
no garden as such, but you will find two benches in the little car park.
Accommodation is provided in ten comfortable bedrooms.

Telephone: 01491 872829.

How to get there: The Miller of Mansfield is situated in Goring's High
Street (B4009), 250 yards east of the Thames bridge. There is a train
service to Goring and Streatley from London (Paddington) and Oxford
twice-hourly from Monday to Saturday, hourly on Sunday. Turn left on
leaving the station and left over the railway bridge into High Street.

Parking: In the hotel's car park or the town car park nearby.
Alternatively, along Thames Road (at its far end), which is off the
High Street between the pub and the river.

Goring Lock.

Length of the walk: 3 miles. Map: OS Landranger 175 Reading, Windsor and surrounding area. A small part of the walk is on OS map 174 Newbury, Wantage and surrounding area (inn GR 598808).

After joining the Thames at Goring Lock (where the activity of boats and boatmen may delay your start!) the walk follows the river upstream for 1¹/₂ miles. It turns 'inland' to Gatehampton Farm, where the farm shop is a welcome halfway house. From here you have a direct route back to Goring, with two possible diversions if you wish to return alongside the river.

The Walk

Turn right on leaving the Miller of Mansfield (or right from Thames Road if you have left your car there) and make your way to the river by branching left over the 'keep clear' road markings and passing Goring Mill. Go left onto the Thames path and stay with this under trees and along meadows for 1¹/₄ miles to a railway arch. From the arch continue forward one more field length to a gate and alongside a fence to Ferry Cottage. Leave the river by turning left and crossing a footbridge, then continue 'inland' and join a T-junction after 100 yards. Turn left here and keep forward over a crossing by Kingfisher Cottage. Go only as far as Gatehampton Farm Shop (100 yards), where a signpost points to Goring

(1 mile). Nearby Gatehampton Manor traces its roots back to AD 1086 and is one of three manors known to have existed in the Goring area.

Turn left into the metalled drive (or via the farm shop if making a purchase or just 'looking') and right on arrival at a concrete farm crossing. As you make that second turn notice the magnificent barn with its horse and plough weather vane. After walking a fenced track between meadows and passing under a railway arch, go through a gate and immediately cross a service track to another gate. Then cut off a large corner of a field by aiming for yet another gate along the adjacent field edge (310°). By walking in the direction of the right-hand extremity of a distant hillside, you should arrive at the correct point. Once through that third gate go straight on along a wide track between fields.

Although the direct route back to Goring's High Street is straight on through a metal kissing gate and along a residential street (with some very fine houses), you could return via the Thames path by going left into one of two linking paths hereafter. There is one such path about 50 yards beyond the gate (signposted where the street-proper begins) and another by 'Little Norfolk' later on. The direct route will take you past another very fine pub – the John Barleycorn – and straight on back to the Miller of Mansfield.

South Moreton
The Crown

As with nearby North Moreton, this is a village where the old is mixed with the new. It has enjoyed a prosperous past, supporting no less than four manor houses in pre-Norman times. In more recent years it was noted for its large paper mill, and Paper Mill Lane near the Crown is a reminder of this.

In addition to a comprehensive regular menu, there are three blackboard lists – snacks, main meals and vegetarian. The snacks include ploughman's lunches, burgers, filled jacket potatoes and sandwiches. Examples of vegetarian meals are broccoli and walnut cheesebake and cauliflower cheese. Spaghetti bolognese, chicken Kiev, lasagne and fresh fish could be among the main meals. There is a special children's menu (a selection of savoury dishes, each with potato 'smiles'!) and a good choice of sweets. Everything is home-made and is available seven days a week from 12 noon to 2 pm and 7 pm to 9.30 pm. At Sunday lunchtime the main meals menu is given over to the traditional roast, while the other menus remain.

There are five real ales, including a guest which is changed every two weeks. Strongbow cider and Heineken and Stella lagers are on draught and there is a good choice of wines by the glass or bottle – from France,

Germany, Bulgaria and Australia. Opening hours are from 11 am to 3 pm and 5.30 pm to 11 pm on Monday to Saturday, and from 12 noon to 3 pm and 7 pm to 10.30 pm on Sunday. Prospective customers at the Crown are left in no doubt as to the welcome offered to families – a clear sign outside says so! And since the pub's resident hounds are out of sight during opening hours, your well-behaved dog is also welcome inside.
Telephone: 01235 812262.

How to get there: South Moreton is signposted from the A417 (1³/₄ miles via Aston Tirrold), midway between Streatley and Harwell. It is also signposted from the A4130 Hithercroft roundabout (not the Slade End roundabout) by Wallingford's Industrial Centre. The pub is in South Moreton's High Street.

Parking: In one of the two pub car parks or along the High Street nearby.

Length of the walk: 2¹/₂ miles. Map: OS Landranger 174 Newbury, Wantage and surrounding area (inn GR 561882).

A walk to please everyone! It visits the sister village of North Moreton, where there are two more pubs and some of the most attractive timber-framed cottages in the county, and where the parish church retains an outstanding 13th-century stained glass window. It twice crosses the main line to the West – doubtless to the delight of railway enthusiasts – and samples the simple pleasures of Oxfordshire's countryside.

The Walk
Go along the drive to the left of the Crown (Crown Lane), passing the pub's rear car park and keeping forward along a terraced track beyond the entrance to Tendercroft. Soon turn right with the track (ignore a stile at the corner) and head towards a railway arch, which you will not see until you are closer. On emerging from the arch turn right and go along a field edge, with the railway embankment on the right. Pass through a gap to the next field and cross this half-left to a stile and river footbridge on the far side – but don't go over the bridge. Stay on the left bank of the river and follow its meanderings to another footbridge, while enjoying a view of the Sinodun Hills half-left. Ignore this footbridge also, and veer left away from the river to another, smaller, footbridge (which you should **not** ignore!) giving access to the next field.
    Go left immediately in this next field, then soon turn right from the field corner and walk parallel to both the trees and a brook. When the brook appears to turn left (it is in fact a branch) keep forward between the fields to a two-pole electricity pylon. Enter the next field

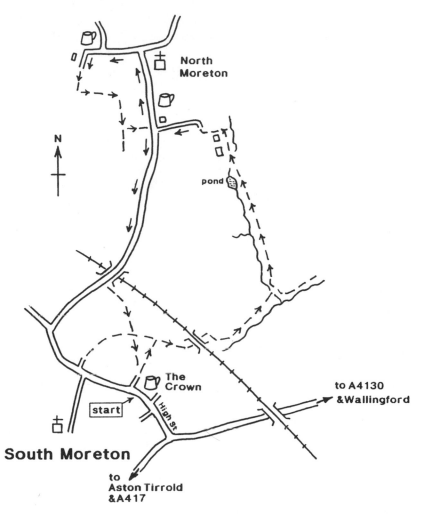

North
Moreton

N

pond

The
Crown

start

High St

South Moreton

to A4130
&Wallingford

to
Aston Tirrold
&A417

here (at a corner), and with a scattering of trees and the brook on the left, eventually arrive at a pond and a number of large commercial greenhouses. Walk between the greenhouses and the brook (which has gone underground only to reappear on the right) and turn sharp left immediately beyond a large modern barn. This will place you on a concrete drive, where you should turn right. Soon go left with the drive and pass between houses to the road by North Moreton's village hall.

Turn right into the road and go past the Bear public house to the T-junction at the village centre. There are many lovely old houses here, also a magnificent tithe barn with attractive herringbone brickwork.

Your next move is to turn left at the T-junction, but a short excursion to the right will take you to the parish church – an absolute 'must' if you are at all interested in early stained glass windows! The South Chapel is lit by 'one of the finest examples for its period in Europe'. The glass dates back to 1299 and still retains its richness of colour.

Back at the T-junction turn left (relative to your earlier direction) and go uphill along a raised pavement to the Queen Victoria pub. Pass to the left of the pub (by West End Cottage) and soon turn left into a short concrete drive parallel to a line of bungalows. Keep forward alongside a paddock fence and hedge, and when the hedge turns left go with it along a wide, grassy swathe in the direction of the houses. The green waymark arrows hereabouts mark the route of a 'licensed' horseway, which is not always coincident with a public right of way. Turn right out of the next corner and go uphill between a fenced meadow and a large field for 150 yards to a wide (fenced) branch on the left. This branch soon takes you over a crossing and along a grass track between hedges, thence to the road opposite the village hall.

Turn right at the road and follow this uphill between the houses and into open country – where there is a wide view of the Thames Valley, including Wallingford with its prominent factory tower. On arrival at the railway crossing turn left immediately beyond the bridge parapet and walk between the railway cutting and the allotment gardens. Soon turn half-right with the path (moving away from the railway) and go straight on between paddocks towards the Crown pub, eventually joining Crown Lane where the walk started.

11 Crowmarsh Gifford
The Bell

With the advent of a modern river bridge upstream from Crowmarsh, traffic passing the Bell has been much reduced over recent years. An inn at least as far back as 1742, it has undergone a number of changes. What was once a cottage is now the public bar, and the taproom has been transformed into a comfortable lounge. In winter this is a cosy place to be – the huge pile of logs waiting in readiness by the fireplace bears witness to this. The paddock has also been transformed, and accommodates cars rather than horses!

The Bell offers a wide range of home-cooked food. Included on the regular menu are starters, cold platters (ploughman's lunches, salads, baguettes and sandwiches) and filled jacket potatoes. Home-made pie of the day (of which the Bell is justly proud) heads the list of hot dishes, followed by steaks, fish (scampi and cod), jumbo sausages and lasagne. You will also find a specials board and a selection of sweets. Since sandwiches and baguettes are made only from daily fresh bread, they are not available on Sunday. With this exception, a full menu is offered every day – Monday to Saturday from 11.30 am to 2 pm and 5.30 pm to 9 pm, and Sunday from 12 noon to 2 pm and 7 pm to 9 pm.

The real ales include Morland Original and Old Masters. Strongbow cider is on draught, as well as Foster's and Stella lagers, Guinness and Murphy's stout. Opening hours are 'all day' (11 am to 11 pm) on Monday to Saturday, and from 12 noon to 3 pm and 7 pm to 10.30 pm on Sunday. Families are welcome here and would feel at home in the lounge. In summer the children will find happy distraction on the play apparatus outside. Dogs may only be taken into the garden. Bed and breakfast accommodation is available.

Telephone: 01491 835324.

How to get there: The Bell is situated in The Street, ⅓ mile east of the **old** Wallingford river bridge. The Street runs to the west of the Crowmarsh roundabout, where the A4130 and A4074 meet.

Parking: In the pub's large car park or in the roadside layby west of the nearby roundabout opposite the church (not the A4130 roundabout). Otherwise, you could use the pay and display car park on the Crowmarsh bank of the river. Starting from here would reduce the walking distance by ½ mile.

Length of the walk: 2½ miles (or 4 miles if you want to visit Benson Lock). Map: OS Landranger 175 Reading, Windsor and surrounding area (inn GR 617892).

After going over Wallingford's medieval bridge, this easy walk follows a short stretch of the river Thames. There is a 1½ mile option to visit Benson Lock, then it leaves the river and heads towards Wallingford's castle and the attractive old town centre, before recrossing the bridge.

The Walk
After turning right from the Bell, go straight on over the roundabout. As you head towards the bridge, notice some fine houses here and there, in particular the timber-framed terrace, numbered 19. Notice also the parish church of St Mary Magdalene, with its tiny windows, wooden bellcote and sealed-up south doorway. If you go round to the north side of the church you will see a door with holes reputed to be from gun shots during the Civil War. Believe that if you will! The bridge dates back to the 13th century and has no less than 19 arches, a fact that may not be apparent as you cross it to the opposite bank. Once there, turn right into Castle Lane by the Town Arms pub and soon join a path on the right by Munts Mill. This passes between brick walls and leads to the river bank, where there are seats for you to rest a while whilst enjoying the view.

Stay with the towpath for ½ mile until you arrive at a pair of gates and an old metal fence separating one field from the next – in line with a half-timbered boathouse on the opposite bank. If you feel energetic you

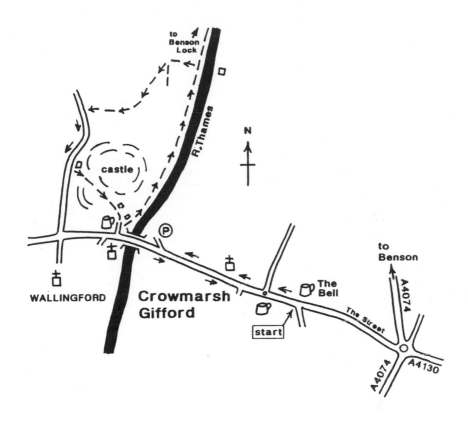

could now extend the walk by a total of 1½ miles by continuing along the towpath as far as Benson Lock (or as far as you like!) and coming back to this point.

Whatever your choice, leave the river by following the metal fence (with the fence on the left) into the field's left-hand corner, where there is a pair of metal gates and a stile, also a fenced farm track (which you should ignore) running between fields. Go over the stile and turn left into a hedge-lined track. As you walk the track you will have the first intimations of Wallingford's castle ruins. In a nutshell, the castle was built by William the Conquerer and destroyed by Oliver Cromwell – with 600 years of chequered history in between!

You will then pass through a cemetery along its drive to the A329 road. Turn left at the road (crossing to the pavement for safety) and follow its right and left bends. When you are 50 yards beyond the second bend, go left onto a wide footpath beyond an isolated house, numbered 24 (whatever happened to nos 1 to 23?). The path runs between brick walls and under an archway to a Castle Grounds entrance gate. If the

Wallingford Castle ruins.

grounds are closed you must settle for a glimpse of the ruins by peering over the walls. Continuing along the path, soon turn right by farm buildings and follow a short tarmac drive back to the Town Arms and Wallingford Bridge. For Crowmarsh and the Bell cross the bridge and walk straight on.

Places of interest nearby

Since this has been a shortish walk you may have sufficient reserves of energy to visit *Wallingford's old town centre*. For this, turn right from the Town Arms into the High Street. The Market Place is a particular attraction, with its elegant 17th-century Town Hall and Corn Exchange. Railway enthusiasts may wish to visit the *Cholsey and Wallingford Railway*, 'one of the oldest surviving GWR branch lines in the Thames Valley', which is 15 minutes walk from the town centre. Operating days are normally two Sundays each month and bank holidays, April to September. The pleasant *Castle Gardens* are open from 10 am to 6 pm in summer (April to October) and from 10 am to 3 pm in winter.

Berrick Salome
The Chequers

With its tall, classical proportions, the Chequers pub is a prominent feature in this peaceful Oxfordshire village. There is no formality inside, however, where a friendly conviviality is the order of the day. The menu introduces itself with a variety of 'Starters and Light Bites' and goes on to 'Quick and Easy', which includes ploughman's lunches, off the bone ham and Chequer's Brunch – with enough calories to propel you round the walk many times over! The dozen or so items under the 'Specialities of the House' heading will keep even the most choosy customer happy. There are steaks, barbecued rack of ribs, mushroom stroganoff and much more. Children have their own menu and there is a good choice of sweets. All food is home-made using fresh vegetables (there's not a frozen pea in sight) and is available on Tuesday to Sunday from 12 noon to 2 pm and 7 pm to 10 pm (7.30 pm to 9 pm on Sunday). Since no food is offered on Monday at lunchtime or in the evening, you could bring your own picnic on that day for eating in the garden – assuming you are buying drinks. Naturally, this does not apply to bank holiday Mondays, when pub food is available as normal.

This being a Brakspear pub, two of the Henley brewery's real ales are on offer – Ordinary and Special. Heineken and Stella lagers, Strongbow

cider, Murphy's stout and Guinness are all on draught. Opening hours are from 11 am to 3 pm and 6 pm to 11 pm on Monday to Saturday, and from 12 noon to 3 pm and 7 pm to 10.30 pm on Sunday. Families are welcome inside and are often to be seen here. In favourable weather children will much prefer the garden, with its good assortment of play equipment. Your dog may be taken into the bar (if kept on a lead) but not into the restaurant area.
Telephone: 01865 891279.

How to get there: Berrick Salome is signposted from the B4009 1½ miles east of Benson and from the A329 between Warborough and Stadhampton. Whichever route you take, simply drive straight on until you see the Chequers.

Parking: In the pub's own car park. Alternatively, you can leave your car by the parish church a short distance into the walk – but not when services are about to commence!

Length of the walk: 2½ miles. Map: OS Landranger 164 Oxford and surrounding area (inn GR 622944).

Since no walk from Berrick Salome would be complete without calling at the parish church, this interesting building is included near the start. Thereafter the walk performs a half-circuit of the village before ascending the slope to Ewe Farm – where the view across the Thames Valley is one of the best you'll find anywhere!

The Walk

From the Chequers car park turn right and go along the drive signposted to the church, ignoring a bridleway leaving from the left en route. When you see the church for the first time I'm sure you will be as surprised and delighted as I was. To one commentator it is reminiscent of 'a Victorian ornament for a cottage mantelpiece'! Inside, a marvellous complexity of roof timbers (dated 1615) overlooks a chancel and transept furnished with tiny oak pews. There is also an unusual balcony – clearly dated 1676 – and a Saxon font that could be 1,000 years old.

Go over a stile opposite the churchyard gate and cross a field to another stile (230°). This second stile is to the right of a cottage and may not be apparent until you are almost there. On arrival at a road (by a telephone box) turn left and follow this to a road junction – passing the grand entrance to Caer Urfa, guarded by foxes, it seems! From the junction turn right into the metalled drive to Lower Farm (labelled as a footpath) and go along this to a footbridge on the right at the halfway point. Passing between ponds, enter a field and cross this half-left to a

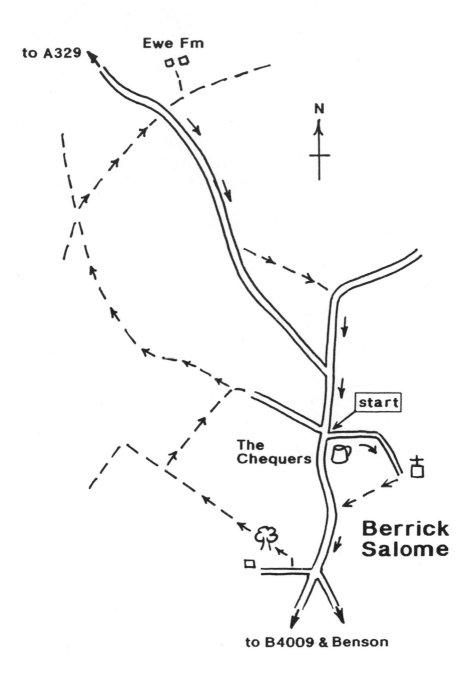

to A329

Ewe Fm

N

start

The Chequers

Berrick Salome

to B4009 & Benson

St Helen's church, Berrick Salome.

stile under conifer trees. Follow the path through the trees and go over a footbridge and stile on the far side, then walk the left-hand edge of a field for 130 yards and cross another stile. Continue in the same direction, but now along the right-hand edge of a field, with a hedge on the right. The view to your left includes the two peaks of the distant Sinodun Hills and the cooling towers at Didcot.

Now don't walk all the way to the field corner, but go through a tall metal gate on the right. This is about 120 yards before the corner and leads into the adjacent field (the same one as previously). Cross this towards a gate a little left of houses (about 40°), passing a fenced enclosure en route. For a really short walk, you could go through the gate and soon arrive back at the pub! For the complete walk, however, turn sharp left a few yards before the gate and walk between a hedge and a cattle trough to a stile and footbridge (to the left of a pond) placed centrally at the far end of the field. Cross the next field half-left (270°) to another stile and footbridge and turn right immediately, following a hedge and ditch on the right.

Stay with the ditch all the way to another footbridge and go forward over this into the next field. When you are about halfway along the field edge turn right at a waymark post and enter the field on the right, going over the ditch in the process. Cross this field towards farm buildings (50°), and enjoy a superb view of the Thames Valley as you go. This should take you up to the road opposite the rough drive to Ewe Farm. By going forward along the drive to its summit you can enjoy an even better view – a 180° span from the Chiltern Hills (including the M40 cutting) to the Oxfordshire Downs.

Back at the road go downhill for 1/4 mile to a footpath signpost on the left. From here cut off a large corner of a field by aiming for a stile and footbridge one third of the way along its lower edge, measured from the road end (120° – in the direction of the signpost finger). Continue in the same direction in the next field towards a metal farm gate near the lower left-hand corner, and join a road. Turn right at the road and follow it back to the Chequers.

13 Steventon
The Fox Inn

Steventon's chief claim to fame is in its medieval stone causeway and its many fine old houses. The Fox Inn can also claim popularity – for its comfortable atmosphere, its wide range of food, and its welcome to families. The bar menu should satisfy the most choosy of customers. There are sandwiches (no less than 14 varieties), ploughman's lunches, salads, filled jacket potatoes, toasties and omelettes. More substantial meals include lasagne, steak pie, ham off the bone, plaice, cod, steaks and mixed grill. In addition to the bar menu, a good-value three-course lunch is available on Sundays. Meals are served every day from 12 noon to 2 pm and 6 pm to 9.30 pm (7 pm to 9 pm on Sunday evenings). Non-smokers will welcome the fact that one of the dining areas is designated a smoke-free zone.

There are usually about five real ales (Morland and a guest), as well as Foster's, Kronenbourg and Stella lagers. The two draught ciders are Scrumpy Jack and Red Rock. Opening hours from Monday to Saturday are 11 am to 2.30 pm and 5 pm (6 pm on Saturday) to 11 pm. Sunday hours differ very slightly from the norm and are 12 noon to 2.30 pm and 7 pm to 10.30 pm. Overnight accommodation is available.

Telephone: 01235 821228.

How to get there: Steventon is on the B4017 some 4 miles south of Abingdon and is bypassed by the A34(T). Leave the A34(T) along the A4130 (signposted to Steventon) and turn right into the B4017 after ¹/₂ mile. (Note that older maps may show the A34(T) running through the centre of Steventon.) Bus 35A between Didcot Parkway railway station and Oxford (Queen Street) calls at Steventon hourly from Monday to Saturday (only). The Fox Inn is close to the railway bridge in Steventon's High Street (B4017).

Parking: In the inn's car park or along the High Street.

Length of the walk: 3¹/₂ miles. Map: OS Landranger 164 Oxford and surrounding area (inn GR 472918).

A walk that is part urban and part rural. The rural part follows the Ginge and East Hendred Brooks through a series of meadows, while the urban part includes The Causeway. This raised walkway is overlooked by a number of very old houses, some of which are owned by the National Trust. Train enthusiasts will be delighted to know that the main line to the West is never far away, and that the walk crosses its route twice!

The Walk

Cross the road from the Fox and go over the railway bridge (the pavement is safer on that side) to a wide drive on the right, commencing where the parapet ends. The drive runs parallel with the railway for a short distance before veering left. It turns right, then left and joins Stocks Lane, along which can be seen a level crossing. Turn left into Stocks Lane and immediately right into Castle Street. Walk the length of Castle Street and turn right where it becomes Mill Street, ignoring a bridleway signpost at the corner, on the left. After crossing Ginge Brook turn left immediately on a grassy footpath running between the brook (and its waterfall) and a garden. The path soon turns right to a footbridge, giving access to a field. Follow the left-hand edge, parallel with the brook, to a stile in the far left-hand corner, then continue forward a few more yards to the precincts of Hill Farm.

Turn right into the farm drive and soon left to a stile and gate between buildings. A signpost points the way ('Hendreds 1') while the farm drive itself heads back to Steventon. Your route is now more or less straight on through a whole series of meadows, extending in total for about ¹/₂ mile, with the deeply meandering East Hendred Brook keeping company all the way. You must ignore a signpost and stile on the left after 300 yards (measured from the previous farm) and continue forward until you arrive at the far end of the last meadow. At this point the brook is about 50 yards to your left and a stile takes you into a cultivated field ahead.

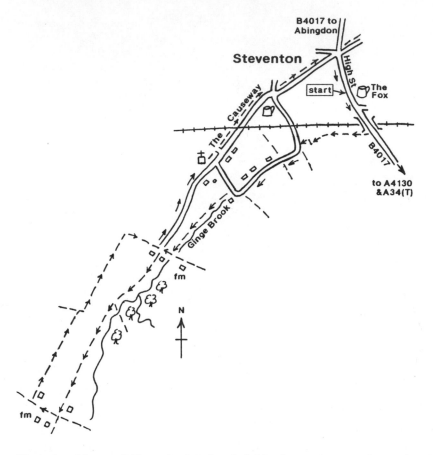

You should now follow the left-hand field edge – along with overhead power lines – to a farmhouse at Wood's Farm.

From the farmhouse turn right into a rough farm drive and, passing two black metal barns, go only as far as another farmhouse on the right, where the drive continues forward through a gate. Turn right immediately beyond the house and its garden and soon cross the fields at right angles to the drive, along a slightly raised grass bank. Since you are now heading back to Steventon, you may well notice the parish church directly ahead – at some distance. Cross a ditch from the far end of the grass bank and go through a pedestrian gate to the right-hand meadow. Passing an electricity pole on the left quite soon, follow the left-hand edge of the meadow to a pair of gates in the far corner.

From the gates turn right into a field track, soon going left with it and resuming your previous direction. The track runs between a ditch and a

Priory Cottage, Steventon.

cultivated field and eventually turns right, taking you back to Hill Farm. When you are at the centre of the farm complex turn left and follow the metalled drive to the parish church.

Opposite the church is Manor Farm, with marvellous colouring in its brickwork. Alongside the farm stands a fine timber barn on brick arches – obviously well cared-for. At the east gate of the churchyard can be seen the beginnings of The Causeway, a raised stone pavement extending for almost 1 mile through Steventon. It has been suggested that this pavement was laid down about 700 years ago and that it enabled access to both the church and Steventon's priory during times of flood. You will see part of the priory on the right very soon, a superb timber-framed building where Mill Street joins The Causeway. Originally a monastic building, it was given to the National Trust in 1939 and is now divided into two dwellings – The Priory and Priory Cottage.

As you walk along The Causeway the next building of note is the Old Vicarage. Also in the care of the National Trust, this splendid house has origins in the 13th and 15th centuries. At the level crossing you are back in the 20th century, and at the road junction ahead the North Star pub confesses to being a 'half-way inn between London and Bristol'. This is an interesting old pub and well worth a closer look, especially inside. The sign is that of George Stephenson's famous locomotive, the North Star.

Continuing along The Causeway, eventually arrive back at the High Street, taking due note of more fine houses as you go. Turning right into the High Street, you will find the Fox Inn along on the left.

14 Garsington
The Three Horseshoes

Overlooking Oxford and the Thames Valley from a height of 300 ft and more, Garsington has earned the name 'Village of Views'. Though not as ancient as the truncated (and mended) 13th-century cross nearby, the Three Horseshoes has commanded the near-summit of the hill since 1812 or earlier. With much of the seating upholstered, today's customers can enjoy the last word in comfort and relaxation, and in winter the warmth of the real log fires. An impressive ship's keel supports part of the ceiling and the walls are hung with numerous early photographs of local residents.

A choice can be made from either the bar snack menu or the full à la carte restaurant menu. The snack menu has a good range of items, including ploughman's lunches, home-made soup, baguettes and toasted sandwiches. There are a variety of filled jacket potatoes, also plaice, scampi, sausages, beefburgers and freshly-cut ham off the bone. Blackboards extend the choice further with a selection of specials, vegetarian dishes and sweets. Both menus are in use every day from 12 noon to 2 pm (3 pm on Sunday) and 7 pm to 9.30 pm (9 pm on Sunday). A roast lunch is served on Sundays.

In addition to a 'guest ale of the month', Morrells Varsity, Best Bitter

and Bass real ales are available, as well as Kronenbourg and Harp lagers and Strongbow cider on draught. Opening hours are from 11 am to 11 pm on Monday to Saturday, and from 12 noon to 3 pm and 7 pm to 10.30 pm on Sunday. Families are welcome in the restaurant area, where smoking is discouraged, but they may prefer the large garden, which has a children's play area. Dogs are not allowed inside.
Telephone: 01865 361395.

How to get there: Garsington is ½ mile or so from the B480, midway between Oxford and Stadhampton. It is clearly signposted from this road. Bus 101 from Oxford (Queen Street) calls at Garsington two-hourly from Monday to Saturday (only). The pub is in The Green (no green in sight!) a short distance from the war memorial.

Parking: In the pub's large car park or along The Green nearby.

Length of the walk: 3 miles. Map: OS Landranger 164 Oxford and surrounding area (inn GR 582024).

An exceptional walk for vistas and fine buildings. It enjoys views of Oxford city to the west and the hilltop village of Cuddesdon to the east. It passes Garsington's medieval cross and the 19th-century Old School House, and visits the parish church. It calls at 18th-century Denton House at the turning-point and Garsington's manor house towards the end.

The Walk
On leaving the Three Horseshoes, turn left into The Green and, passing the Old School House (built in 1840), go straight on downhill along Southend to St Mary's church. Enter the churchyard from the lychgate and circulate clockwise around the church to a short flight of steps and a gate on the right. This will place you in a meadow, which you should cross in the direction of a thatched cottage. A gate will direct you between stone walls to the right of the cottage and onto a road. Cross to a stile on the left side of Knoll House (no 20) and go forward in a sloping meadow to a stile in the top right-hand corner. Keeping forward again, soon go downhill past an old orchard to another stile. Taking your aim from the gas holders in distant Oxford, cross the upper end of a large field and turn half-right (not straight on) from a hedge-gap and ditch on the far side. Climb the hill towards the houses on the summit (50°) and make your exit by passing between gardens to a road.

Turn left at the road and pass the Red Lion pub, before going downhill to an unusual feature – two pavements, one above the other. Take the upper pavement and go with it around the garden of Garsington House, passing through a gate and crossing a stile in the process. On entering a

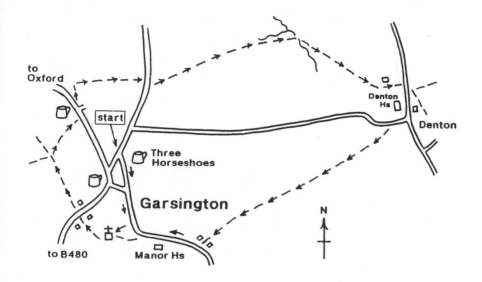

field, follow the right-hand hedge to the hedge-corner and keep straight on uphill to a stile at the top (50°). Keep straight on again across the next field to a stile, and along a short path to another road.

Turn right at the road and cross this to a rough drive (signposted as a footpath) after 35 yards. The drive passes between houses and garages to a stile (not visible until you are close to it) which gives entry to a field. Cross the short right-hand edge of the field downhill to a further stile and enter another, larger, field. Visibility permitting, you will see the hilltop village of Cuddesdon directly ahead. It looks worth a visit! Follow the right-hand edge of the field for about 100 yards and cross a stile on the right giving access to the adjacent field. Reverting to your previous direction, walk the left-hand edge of this field, with a hedge on your left, to a stile in its far corner. Continue forward in the next field, crossing to a stile and footbridge near the field's lowest point (90°).

Turn half-right from the footbridge and go uphill to the left-hand of two electricity poles which stand in the field. On passing the pole, keep straight on to a stile and cross a meadow to another stile in the far corner, aiming all the while at the cube-shaped building topped with a lantern and weather vane – part of the Denton House estate. The Gothic window incongruously placed in the garden wall came from Brasenose College Chapel, Oxford. It was brought here in the 1840s following restoration of the chapel. The observant in your party may discover two further, smaller, windows hereafter!

Soon cross another stile and go along a grassy path to the road. Turn right at the road and pass between Denton House and its farm buildings

The Old School, Garsington.

to a road junction. Although the house contains parts dating back to the 16th century, it is essentially of the 18th. The date on the rainwater heads seems to indicate remodelling of the house in 1757. It is not normally open to the public. Turn right at the road junction and walk the length of a stone wall to where it terminates. Leave the road here by turning half-left (with respect to your direction along the road) into a signposted path (230°). Note that the signpost may not be pointing in the correct direction!

You now have a straight, well-used path to take you gradually uphill through a succession of fields to the summit, passing a small gravel pit and (later) a cattle trough en route. You will eventually (½ mile from Denton) pass between houses before joining the road at Garsington. A right turn into the road, followed by a close encounter with the Manor House (where you should use the raised pavement for safety), and you will soon be back at the Three Horseshoes. The manor is not open to the public, except on certain days under the National Gardens Scheme.

15 Old Marston
The Bricklayers Arms

In medieval times Marston (or Marsh Town) consisted of no more than a few cottages and a church. It existed on what was in effect an island within the swampy environs of the river Cherwell. The river is now under better control and the village has extended its borders to include houses old and new. The pub owes its name to the brick-making industry that existed here in earlier times.

Today the Bricklayers Arms is a model of comfort and friendliness, and a marvellous place to enjoy good food. You can choose from an extensive blackboard menu ranging from simple snacks to main meals. There are ploughman's lunches, filled jacket potatoes, omelettes and soup. Examples from the main meals are broccoli and cauliflower cheesebake, steak and kidney pie and baked trout. Tagliatelle bolognese expresses an Italian slant to the menu, while giant Yorkshire puddings with spicy sausage and gravy otherwise keep it firmly in Britain! Children have their own special menu.

From March to September inclusive the pub is open for food and drink from 11.30 am to 11 pm on Monday to Saturday, and from 12 noon to 3 pm and 7 pm to 10.30 pm on Sunday. From October to February the times are 11.30 am to 3.30 pm and 6.30 pm to 11 pm, with Sunday opening remaining unchanged. There is a full menu throughout.

The real ales are Wadworth 6X and Tetley. Olde English cider is on draught, as are Castlemaine XXXX and Lowenbräu lagers. The pub goes out of its way to welcome families. If the weather keeps the children inside there is plenty to occupy them, including board games, crayons and cuddly toys. Dogs are welcome but should be kept on a lead.

Telephone: 01865 250177.

How to get there: Old Marston is $1/4$ mile from the A40(T) ring road north of Oxford. From the A40(T) take the road signposted to Marston, then follow signs to Old Marston. The pub is situated opposite Old Marston's parish church in Church Lane.

Parking: In the pub's car park or along Elsfield Road by the parish church.

Length of the walk: 3 miles. Map: OS Landranger 164 Oxford and surrounding area (inn GR 527089).

The principal attraction of this walk is the delightful river Cherwell where it flows near Oxford's University Parks. It crosses Wolfson College nature reserve where the north and south meads are 'relics of a medieval farming system' and an important area for wildlife. The meads and the riverside path can become very muddy after periods of wet weather so it's a good idea to have your wellington boots at the ready.

The Walk

From the Bricklayers Arms go along the narrow lane between the churchyard and a high stone wall. This is Ponds Lane and leads directly to the Manor House and Cromwell's House at a road junction. When built, these houses were of one entity; and it was here, in the Civil War, that the Royalist surrender of Oxford was negotiated. Go right with the road and first left where a sign proclaims the Victoria Arms. Cross a stile on the right quite soon and walk the entire length of a long meadow. This meadow is linked to the next by a narrow neck of grass, which takes you within sight of both the river Cherwell and the Victoria Arms.

Climb a stile on the left just beyond the pub (which is on the left); then cross the grass alongside the pub's terrace to a footbridge opposite. The footbridge connects with a good path under trees, and this in turn leads to Marston Ferry Road. Cross the road to a stile opposite and walk the right-hand edge of a field, with the river Cherwell running parallel on the right. The prominent building in view on the hilltop to your left is the renowned John Radcliffe Hospital. A stile and gate near the far end of the field coincides with a bend in the river and a sign announces the

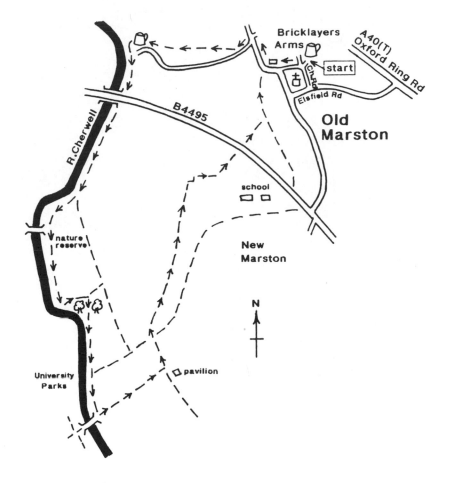

Wolfson College Nature Reserve.

Go half-right with the river towards, but not over, a private footbridge to Wolfson College. An information board at this point explains in some detail the importance of the reserve. Having passed the footbridge go through to the next meadow from the nearby corner. Follow the river through this and two more meadows, eventually to a stile and footbridge under a stand of tall trees. Turn left immediately from the footbridge, leaving the river bank and following a brook on the left. Bear right after a few yards and cross another footbridge, soon emerging from the trees and rejoining the river.

After ¼ mile a steeply arched footbridge crosses the river Cherwell (which should not be confused with a brook crossed earlier) and links

Cromwell's House.

our path with the University Parks opposite – a pleasant diversion, but not on our route. Turn left on arrival at the footbridge and walk away from the river along a wide path between a brook and a line of tall trees. After 300 yards, and when close to a sports pavilion, turn left at a T-junction in the path; then walk between hedges (there is a sports field on the right) to another T-junction. Keep forward here by crossing a footbridge and entering a large meadow. Cross the meadow half-right (20°) to a stile about 80 yards left of the far right-hand corner.

Cross the next meadow to a stile and footbridge opposite and continue forward along the right-hand edge of another meadow, with a hedge and sports field on the right. Beyond a cattle trough in the far corner turn right into a short concrete drive and left with it almost immediately. The concrete soon terminates and places you in the corner of a long meadow. Your next objective is a stile (as yet unseen) in the diagonally opposite corner of the meadow. The correct route to this is by following the right-hand hedge (ie turning right from the concrete) until you are a short distance from the far right-hand corner, then turning left across the meadow to that stile – which should not be confused with a wide hedge-gap nearby.

Having crossed the stile and entered a cultivated field, cut off a small corner of the field by walking half-right towards a footpath signpost. Cross a cycleway and the Marston Ferry Road to a stile opposite and strike across a field at right angles to the road, aiming for a gap and signpost on the opposite side (40°). This is in the direction of Old Marston's church tower (which may be obscured by trees) and places you on a bridleway behind the houses. Turn left into this and shortly find yourself in the road opposite Cromwell's House. Turn right into the road and first left for the pub.

Places of interest nearby
Old Marston's 12th-century parish church is just across the road from the Bricklayers Arms. Among its 'treasures' is a delicately carved Jacobean pulpit and a wall painting (the royal arms of Queen Anne) above the chancel arch. The south aisle has a particularly fine timber roof.

16 Cumnor
The Vine

The date '1743' on the façade of the Vine leaves us in little doubt as to the age of this fine building. It shares this hilltop village of Cumnor (the one-time 'Cumar's hill-slope') with many equally splendid stone-built houses. The stone walls of the inn remain visible inside, as a backcloth to the comfortable seating of the lounge and the traditional settles in the public bar. On a fine day the garden is a good place to be – with its lawn, pond and fountain, and its well-kept shrubbery.

To say that the Vine specialises in fish is no exaggeration, sometimes as many as ten varieties, each cooked to its own special recipe and using fresh (unfrozen) fish. There is an extensive choice of pasta meals, stirfry dishes and steaks, in addition to a selection of 'lunchtime rolls', ploughman's lunches and sweets. Food hours are straightforward – 12.30 pm to 2.15 pm and 6.30 pm to 9.15 pm every day, with a full menu offered throughout.

The real ales are Wadworth 6X, Abbot Ale and Tetley, while the draught cider is Addlestones. There are about seven wines by the glass and three draught lagers, Castlemaine XXXX, Carlsberg Pilsner and Export. Opening hours are from 11 am to 2.30 pm and 6 pm to 11 pm on Monday to Saturday, and from 12 noon to 3 pm and 7 pm to 10.30 pm on Sunday. Children are welcome inside – in the lounge or in the smoke-free conservatory. Dogs may be taken into the public bar if kept on a lead.

Telephone: 01865 862567.

How to get there: Cumnor is bypassed by, and accessed from, the A420(T), 4 miles south-west of Oxford. The Vine is situated in Abingdon Road, the B4017 where it passes one way (south to north) through the village.

Parking: In the pub's own car park or alongside The Old School in Abingdon Road nearby.

Length of the walk: 3½ miles. Map: OS Landranger 164 Oxford and surrounding area (inn GR 462041).

The principal aim of this walk is to visit the Thames-side Farmoor Reservoir, a vast lake providing recreation as well as water. Getting there is by field edges and alongside a Thames-bound brook, with excellent views of the reservoir and the Thames Valley. Returning is by way of Upper Whitley Farm and its attractive farmhouse. The walk concludes at Cumnor's village pond – a good place to relax and feed the ducks.

The Walk

Turning right from the Vine, go downhill to the road junction opposite St Michael's church. Turn right here into Oxford Road and cross this to Denman's Lane, adjacent to a house called Bennetts. Progressing along the lane, you will soon have the fields for company while leaving the houses behind. When you reach a footpath signpost halfway along these fields (and halfway to farm buildings ahead) you should turn half-left in the direction of a line of tall cypress trees (340°). Crossing a track there and continuing forward alongside the trees (with the trees on the right), you will notice that Farmoor Reservoir has come into view.

Bear slightly right when the trees terminate and go downhill on the grass track to a stile and gate at the near corner of a wood. With the wood now on your right, continue downhill along a field edge and go through a farm gate near the bottom. When the wood comes to an end keep straight on, under power lines and alongside a hedge, to the far right-hand corner of the field. Turn left from the corner and follow the hedge and ditch for about 100 yards until the field edge curves left. Cross the ditch and a pair of stiles here to a corner of the adjacent field. Ignoring a third stile nearby, cross the field in a direction midway between a cattle trough and a distant (on the reservoir) observation tower (290°). When this places you at a stile and gate in the opposite corner, continue forward in the

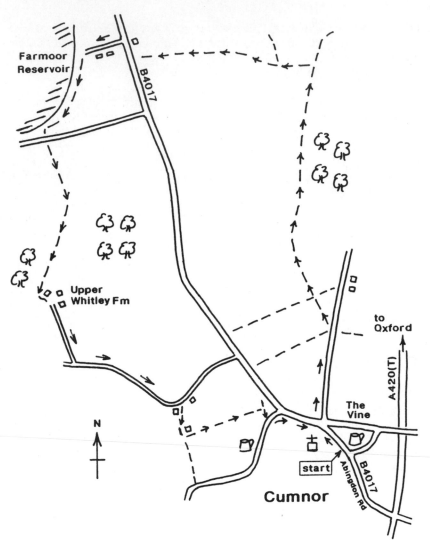

next field, with a hedge and brook on the right (the brook is destined for the Thames) all the way to a road.

Turn right at the road and left after 50 yards into Lower Whitley Road – a drive serving a number of chalet bungalows. Cross a footbridge and stile at the far end of the drive and turn half-left across a meadow, soon joining a perimeter fence of Farmoor Reservoir. Pass between a small plantation and the fence and follow the curve of the reservoir until you meet a stile further round. Walk forward a few more yards between trees and the fence and turn left (not as far as the picnic area), leaving the reservoir behind and crossing a stile to a road.

Cross to the footbridge opposite and go forward along a field edge, with a hedge and ditch on the right. From the turning-point of the hedge (under power lines) turn half-right across this L-shaped field to a stile and footbridge in the opposite hedge. When in the next meadow aim for a stile uphill in the far corner, in line with farm buildings higher up. Continuing uphill, with trees on the right, go through a farm gate and pass to the right of the buildings. Turn left around a large barn and cross a concrete farm track to a stile (of sorts). Walk over the grass for a short distance to the near left-hand corner of a tennis court and go through a gate on the left.

The gate places you in the farm precincts adjacent to a now-occupied outhouse. Turn right from the gate and, passing between the tennis court and the lovely old Upper Whitley Farm house (best seen by looking back), progress uphill on the farm drive. When you meet a T-junction by the entrance to Long Leys Farm, turn left and stay the course for 1/4 mile to the next junction. Turn sharp right here around thatched Leys Cottage (an ideal model for a tea cosy if ever there was) and follow the track to another thatched cottage. Go through a vehicle barrier here and turn left into a recreation ground, making your exit by way of a stile in the far left-hand corner and entering a long meadow. Leave the meadow from the far right-hand corner and turn right, soon joining the road by Cumnor's village pond.

Turn left into the road and right at the T-junction for the Vine. Before returning to the pub do visit St Michael's church. The view from the churchyard is particularly good. Inside the church you will find an unusual oak spiral staircase, also a chained bible of 1611, in a glass case alongside the pulpit. A children's guide to the church is available – informative for adults as well!

⑰ Newbridge
The Rose Revived

Here at Newbridge the Thames joins forces with the lovely river Windrush and flows under a fine 15th-century stone bridge, an idyllic situation shared by two hostelries – the Rose Revived and the Maybush. The Rose Revived equals the bridge in craftsmanship and rivals it in age, at least in part. Today's craftsmen have 'done it proud', especially inside where the extensive ground floor has been separated into small cosy dining areas.

You can choose from the regular menu that is found in other Artist's Fare inns. There are salads and ploughman's lunches, main courses and desserts, tea and coffee. Main courses and specials on the blackboard together add up to an impressive selection of 20 or so items. Children have their own colourful menu with a good choice of items including Sea Stars (fish), Big Bun Burger, Luscious Lasagne and Little Porkies, all backed up with potatoes, chips, peas and beans and followed by puds and iced drinks. Meals are available from 12 noon to 10 pm every day, including Sunday. That's ten hours a day, so you needn't rush back from the walk!

The bar is open from 11 am to 11 pm on Monday to Saturday, and from 12 noon to 3 pm and 7 pm to 10.30 pm on Sunday. There is a

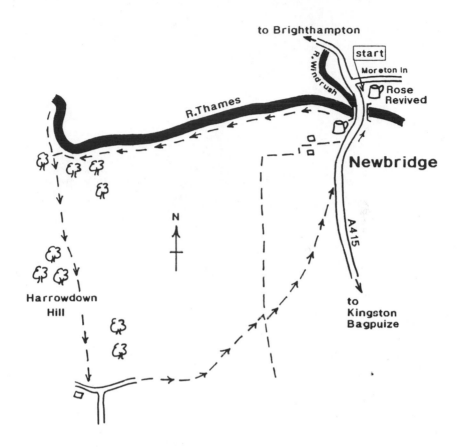

large selection of wines (by the glass or bottle) that you can enjoy with the meal. You may, however, prefer the Morland real ales – Old Masters, Old Speckled Hen, Original Bitter – or the guest ale. Or there are Kronenbourg, Foster's or Stella lagers. Children are welcome inside and are positively encouraged. Well-behaved dogs are also welcome. Accommodation is provided, including special weekend offers. So why not spend the night here and try another walk tomorrow?

Telephone: 01865 300221.

How to get there: The Rose Revived is on the A415 where it crosses the river Thames, midway between Kingston Bagpuize and Brighthampton.

Parking: At the front of the inn or in the large car park at the rear. It is also possible to park in Moreton Lane nearby.

Length of the walk: 3¼ miles. Map: OS Landranger 164 Oxford and surrounding area (inn GR 403015).

After following a mile of this delightful part of the Thames, the walk images the sharp right turn of the river by heading uphill to tree-clad Harrowdown Hill. From here there are superb views across the chequered fields of the Thames Valley, including those that carry the path back to Newbridge.

The Walk

On leaving the Rose Revived your first move is to cross the 15th-century stone bridge, retreating into a recess if traffic is passing. Having done that, turn right onto a path immediately beyond the Maybush pub. This is signposted to Duxford and soon takes you over a footbridge and into a riverside meadow. Follow the river all the way to a gate and into a cultivated field, then go forward to the next field. Here the path leaves the field edge and runs through scrub and trees alongside the river, eventually reaching a footbridge where the river turns sharp right. Having emerged from the trees and crossed the footbridge, turn left along a field edge and go over a stile on the left after 50 yards. A short excursion through the scrub will then place you in a field corner.

Go uphill along the field edge (with a hedge and ditch on the right)

Thames bridge at Newbridge.

to the top right-hand corner. Continue uphill, but now on a grassy track between hedges and soon passing to the left of the trees on Harrowdown Hill. The track descends the hill before running straight and level between tree-rows and shallow ditches. This section terminates at a T-junction where the right-hand branch is labelled 'Tucksmead' (for information only!). Turn left here and continue forward from another junction after a few yards, following power lines along a hard-surfaced track, signposted to Newbridge.

It's not long before the hard surface gives way to grass and ruts (ignore a gate on the left at this point) but quite a long time before the grassy track joins a field. Ignore a footbridge in the field corner and veer slightly left with the hedge, following those power lines to the far end of the field. As the wires decide to head off towards the distant Maybush pub, turn right into a farm track and almost immediately left through a double farm gate. Stay with the left-hand hedge through a sequence of two fields (one short and one long) and on arrival in the third field aim for the far right-hand corner. The narrow extremity of this field is backed by trees, and a stile in the corner connects with a road, the A415. For safety, cross the road to the verge opposite, then turn left and soon enjoy the welcome sight of Newbridge and the Rose Revived.

18 Bampton
The Romany Inn

You cannot fail to be delighted with this marvellous Oxfordshire village. With its rich heritage of stone-built houses you could well imagine yourself in Cotswold country. The 17th-century Romany Inn is a focal point of a popular village pastime – morris dancing. The Bampton Traditional team is based at the inn and an annual village festival attracts visitors and dancers from far and wide. This is a country inn in the best sense of the word, offering appetising food, good ale and comfortable overnight accommodation.

The regular menu extends to no less than six pages, including starters, fish, salads, vegetarian meals, bar snacks (sandwiches and filled jacket potatoes) and sweets. With 25 items in the main courses list, to mention only a selection would do it an injustice. Plaice, scampi, haddock, trout and lemon sole appear under the fish heading, while vegetarian meals amount to at least eight choices, for example vegetarian lasagne, leek and mushroom crustard and vegetable strudel. With the extensive choice of sweets, no one should be at a loss in deciding how to finish off the meal! Food is served from 11.30 am to 2.30 pm and 6 pm to 9.30 pm on Monday to Saturday, and from 12 noon to 2.30 pm and 7 pm to 9.30 pm on Sunday. The full bar menu is in use right the way through.

Families can dine in the restaurant, which is a no-smoking area.

There are four regular real ales (Hook Norton Best and Mild, Archers Village and Morland Original), two guest ales and draught Guinness. Strongbow cider is also on draught, as are Foster's, Carlsberg and Stella lagers. The inn is open from 11 am to 11 pm on Monday to Saturday, and from 12 noon to 3 pm and 7 pm to 10.30 pm on Sunday. Dogs are welcome in the bar, but not in the restaurant. There is a large secluded garden, with a play area for children.

Telephone: 01993 850237.

How to get there: Bampton is 2 miles north of the Thames and 5 miles south-west of Witney, at the point where the A4095 and B4449 meet. The inn is situated in Bridge Street (A4095) near Market Square.

Parking: The inn's own car park is reserved for residents. There is usually plenty of roadside parking space, and yellow lines are a rarity! Bridge Street near the inn is one possibility, as is Market Square or Broad Street nearby. Otherwise, you could park by the parish church, a short distance into the walk.

Length of the walk: 2½ miles. Map: OS Landranger 164 Oxford and surrounding area (inn GR 314031).

The walk commences along one of Bampton's most delightful streets, Church View. It enters the church precincts, which have been likened in atmosphere to a cathedral close, and joins level fields outside the village. Highmoor Brook and Shill Brook provide interest and occasional company before the walk enters its final phase – a long straight track with good views of the church and village. This is an easy walk with absolutely no hills!

The Walk

Cross over from the Romany Inn, turn left, then first right into Church View – signposted to the library and where you have a view of the church, not surprisingly! On arrival at the church go forward on the metalled churchyard path to a gate on the far side. Turn left at the road there and follow it round to the right. Stay on the road for 60 yards to a footpath signpost on the left opposite The Old Vicarage. Go through a metal gate and cross a small paddock at right angles to the road. After entering a meadow turn right immediately and walk behind gardens to a gate and footbridge in the far right-hand corner. From that corner go forward along the right-hand edge of a field, with Highmoor Brook on the right.

After 100 yards or so cross a wide concrete bridge, and then follow the right-hand side of the brook. Looking ahead you will see the

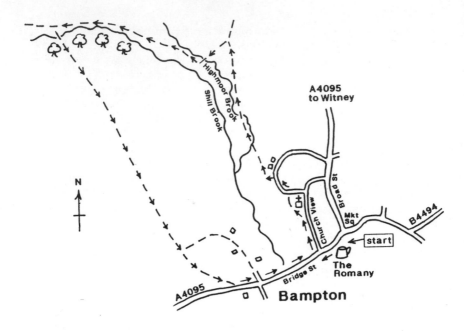

accoutrements of Brize Norton airfield – radar scanners, lighting gantries and the like. After a further 100 yards, and where the brook describes a double S-bend, you should leave the water by aiming across-field to a stile in the hedge on the far side. The stile is about one-third of the way in from the far left-hand corner (350°) and is accompanied by a footbridge. Cross the next field at its narrowest point (that is, slightly left from the previous direction), and on arrival at the hedge opposite turn left across the same field to another footbridge (230°). Turn right immediately after crossing the footbridge and follow Highmoor Brook for about 75 yards (90 man-size paces) to where it curves slightly right, then aim for the far left-hand corner of this long field, where the tall trees terminate (290°).

After crossing a stile in that corner, pass briefly under the trees and enter a field on the right. Going left along the field edge you will be accompanied by a long band of trees, and Shill Brook within the trees. When you are about 25 yards from the far extremity of the tree-line (the present path continues forward) turn left from a waymark post and go under the trees to a footbridge and another field. Now you must aim across this very large field in the direction of an 'island' of low scrub and the much more distant radio masts. This is half-left if your back is to the tree line (150°). All being well, you will eventually pass to the right of a shallow pit (used as a farm dump) before meeting up with a straight hedge-lined track.

The track turning left after ½ mile (in the direction of Bampton's impressively steepled church) is the signal to climb a stile in the bend on the right. After a brief sojourn along a field end you should leave the field via another stile. Your next objective is the square-shaped lodge house in Bampton's Bridge Street two more fields away. For this, take your aim from the waymark arrow on the stile (120°) and, after entering the second field from a footbridge, cross this field to a stile in its opposite left-hand corner.

Turn left into Bridge Street and you are well on your way back to the Romany.

19 Coleshill
The Radnor Arms

From a hill-slope above the river Cole, this delightful National Trust
village overlooks Wiltshire from Oxfordshire. The 17th-century Coleshill
House, once the pivot of the locality and the village, has gone, but the
estate land remains. The Radnor Arms came into being in 1949, in a
building that previously housed the village smithy. The restaurant (in
which families are welcome) is a veritable museum of blacksmith's
artefacts, with numerous horseshoes and tools lining the walls. There
is also a huge anvil – but that's kept on the floor!

The blackboard menu in the bar includes a good range of snacks
and meals, from sandwiches, baguettes and ploughman's lunches to
chicken, broccoli and Stilton pie and Hot Smokie – smoked mackerel
in blue cheese sauce. Gammon, sausages, plaice and scampi are usually
available, also the Radnor Burger, Radnor Pasta, and a choice of sweets.
The restaurant menu includes many of the above items, in addition to
starters and speciality dishes. Meals are served every day from 12 noon
to 2 pm and 7 pm to 10 pm, the bar and restaurant menus being available
throughout.

Real ales are dispensed from barrels behind the bar and usually amount
to about four brews, Flowers Original being the mainstay. Heineken

and Stella lagers and Scrumpy Jack cider are on draught, and there is a selection of good quality wines. The pub is open on Monday to Saturday from 11 am to 2.30 pm (3 pm on Saturday) and 7 pm to 11 pm, and on Sunday from 12 noon to 3 pm and 7 pm to 10.30 pm. Please consult the landlord before bringing your dog into the pub or its garden, as there is already a dog in residence!

Telephone: 01793 762366.

How to get there: The Radnor Arms is easily found – on the B4019 at Coleshill, midway between Faringdon and Highworth. On leaving Faringdon's centre along the B4019 (signposted to Highworth) be careful to turn first right.

Parking: In the pub's own car park or along the roadside (B4019) at the front. You could, alternatively, park by the parish church a little downhill from the pub.

Length of the walk: 2³/₄ miles. Map: OS Landranger 163 Cheltenham and Cirencester area (inn GR 237938).

Choose a clear day for this walk and enjoy wide, sweeping vistas of the Thames Valley. This is a straightforward and uncomplicated walk through farmland owned by The National Trust. It includes a ¹/₄ mile steady field edge climb – the price you pay for one of the views!

The Walk

On leaving the Radnor Arms go along the lane adjacent to the pub's car park. When the lane soon meets another at a road junction, cross to a track opposite, and stay with this for a moment or two (it turns right) before entering the field ahead. Follow the left-hand field edge straight on and slightly uphill. You will pass a tree-shaded pond near the summit of the field, while a marvellous view opens up on the left. The church steeple at Lechlade 4 miles away can be identified (if you have brought your compass, it's at 340°). From the far left-hand corner of this field enter the next one and follow its left-hand edge, eventually descending to a dip under trees. As you emerge from the trees go over a footbridge to a stile and continue straight on.

From the far left-hand corner of the next field go over a stile and forward along a grassy path between a hedge and a wire fence. Research into the use of fertilisers is carried out in the field on the right – this accounts for the numerous water channels, where fertiliser run-off is measured. After crossing a footbridge at the far end of this path, turn left into a field corner. Turn right out of the corner and, resuming your previous direction, follow the field edge for 70 yards to a stile on the

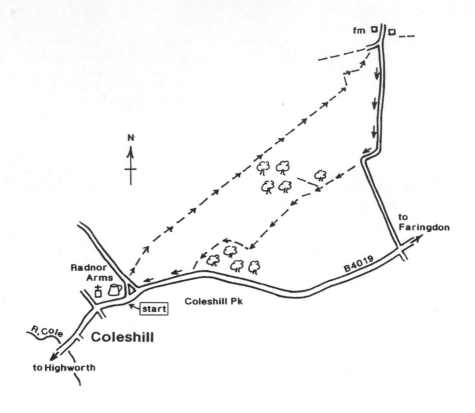

left. Go over the stile and cross a field towards farm buildings situated beyond the field's furthest corner (half-right if your back is to the stile) and go over a stile a little left of that corner. This connects with a farm track on which you should turn right. After 50 yards (when adjacent to the farmyard) turn right into a concrete drive, waymarked as the d'Arcy Dalton Way. Named after Col d'Arcy Dalton, a tireless campaigner for Oxfordshire's footpaths, this 65-mile walk stretches from Wormleighton just beyond the northern extremity of the county to Wayland's Smithy long barrow on the Ridgeway in the south. It was set up in 1985 to celebrate the Golden Jubilee of the Ramblers' Association.

As you leave the farm behind and walk the drive, Badbury Hill will be over to your left. The hill is owned by The National Trust, as is much of the countryside hereabouts. The drive eventually turns right, then left after 90 yards. Leave the drive immediately after that left-hand turn and go into the field on the right. Follow the field's right-hand edge – with a scrubby hedge and trees on the right – all the way to its far right-hand corner, ignoring a right-branching track en route. Cross a footbridge linking this field to the next and launch into a steady uphill climb, once again following a hedge on the right. If you will pause on the way up and turn round, you will have the National Trust's Buscot House in view half-left at 1½ miles.

On arrival at the top corner of the field go through to the field on the right and, with woodland (Cuckoopen Plantation) on your immediate left, follow the curve of the field edge. Two well-known airfields are in view from here – Fairford directly ahead at 6 miles, Brize Norton over your right shoulder at 7½ miles. After entering another field stay with the wood edge for a further 120 yards (where the wood edge goes into the straight) and turn left on a waymarked path. This path takes you through the trees and shortly to a road opposite the National Trust's Coleshill Park.

Coleshill House is no longer. Completed in 1662 and 'one of the most perfect houses in England', it was accidentally burnt down in 1952. During the Second World War it became the headquarters of a British resistance movement, a secret guerrilla army set up in readiness for a possible invasion by Germany.

Turn right at the road and follow this back to the Radnor Arms.

20 Lechlade
The New Inn

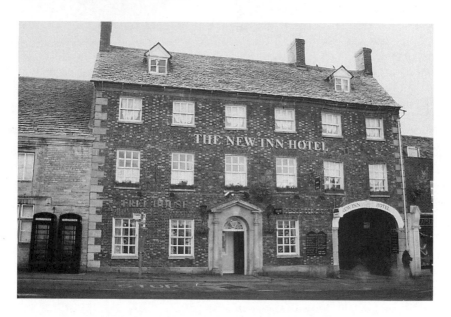

Known as the 'Gateway to the Cotswolds', Lechlade was once an important and prosperous staging post for both road and river traffic. Of the many hostelries that served this coming and going only a handful remain. Numbered among this residue the New Inn claims to have been 'the foremost hotel in Lechlade for more than 250 years, patronised by travellers and poets alike'. The bar of the inn is certainly the place to be if you cherish an ambition to meet the locals. In winter a huge log fire blazes in the hearth, generating a warmth and atmosphere that is second to none. In summer the garden is a strong attraction, since it reaches right down to the river.

The regular bar menu presents a very wide range of choices in six categories: starters, fish, grills, main dishes, vegetarian food and light bites. The specials board adds more than a little daily variety, where examples are beef stew and dumplings, chicken curry and 'sizzler' dishes. With about four varieties of soup, seven of sandwiches and ten sweets, very little is left to chance. Cream teas are available in summer. Meals are served every day from 12 noon to 2 pm and 6.30 pm (7 pm on Sunday) to 9.30 pm. The bar menu has fewer items available at Sunday lunchtime, because of the popularity of the traditional roast on offer.

The inn is open from 11 am to 3 pm and 6 pm to 11 pm on Monday to Saturday, and from 12 noon to 3 pm and 7 pm to 10.30 pm on Sunday – more than enough time to enjoy one of the four real ales (Morland Original, Bass, Arkell's 3B or the guest ale) the Kronenbourg or Carling lagers or the Strongbow cider. Families are welcome in the dining area, where smoking is discouraged. If you wish to take your dog into the bar, please first consult the landlord. Accommodation is available in 27 en-suite rooms separated from, but linked to, the main building. There is a special weekend tariff.

Telephone: 01367 252296.

How to get there: The inn is centrally placed in Lechlade, where the A417 and A361 intersect.

Parking: At the inn's own car park. Other possibilities are the Market Place at the front of the inn (2 hour limit), the public car park along Burford Street, or the roadside in Burford Street (the inn faces this street). If you have come by boat, you could use the inn's very own mooring!

Length of the walk: 3½ miles. Map: OS Landranger 163 Cheltenham and Cirencester area (inn GR 215995).

From the 18th-century Ha'penny Bridge the walk follows the south bank of the Thames to another historic bridge, St John's. It passes the Trout Inn and accompanies the river Leach to Lechlade Mill, returning to Lechlade across fields and through the estate land of Lechlade Manor. A walk full of delight and interest!

The Walk
Turn left on leaving the New Inn and first left into Thames Street, the A361 to Swindon. An attractive terrace of stone cottages precedes Ha'penny Bridge and its tollhouse. The name of the bridge is easily explained – a toll of one half penny was charged at the tollhouse! In order to walk the river bank on the left you will need to cross the bridge and descend a flight of steps on the right, then go under the bridge to the riverside meadow.

The next ¾ mile is uncomplicated – simply follow the river all the way to the next bridge, St John's. There was a bridge here as early as 1229, but what you now see is largely of the 1800s. A lock has been here since 1791 and it is the highest on the Thames. Cross the bridge to the Trout Inn and there (inside or out) indulge in a moment of decision. You have a choice between a straight short-cut path back to Lechlade or the complete walk by way of Lechlade Mill.

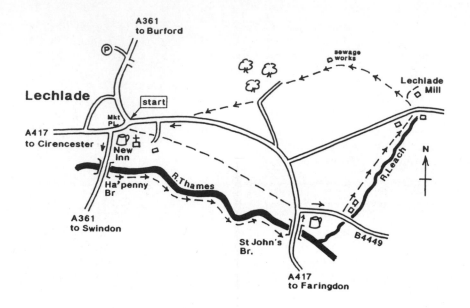

For the short-cut you should cross the footbridge opposite the Kelmscott turn-off (the B4449) and walk the very nice straight path all the way back to Lechlade (but please see my final paragraph!).

For the complete walk turn right into the B4449 and go along this for about 200 yards to the first house on the left (as distinct from the earlier chalet bungalows). Don't go into the field here (as the footpath signpost may suggest) but join a fenced path on the left running between the field and Priory Cottage. After passing the cottage garden go straight on across two small meadows and enter a cultivated field from a stile. With the river Leach in close proximity continue forward, but now along the right-hand edge of the field. Go over a stile in the far right-hand corner of the field and pass to the right of a large industrial building (a wire manufacturer), joining a narrow lane.

For a view of Lechlade Mill and Mill Cottage you should go along the lane a short distance beyond the weight limit sign – but don't forget to come back! Cross the lane from that large building and go forward along a rough drive for a few yards only (by the entrance to Orchard Cottage) until the drive turns right. Cross a field straight on, as indicated by a footpath signpost at the roadside (310°). A stile on the opposite side of the field will place you in the corner of another field. Keep straight on here and follow a wide band of trees and scrub to a stile where the scrub terminates – within 50 yards of a stone barn ahead.

From that stile cross the field on the left to a metal gate in the right-hand border, near a sewage farm (260°). This gate, as you will

The river Thames and Lechlade.

discover, leads into the sewage farm – and you will be delighted to know that your route is not through it but forward along a concrete drive. When the drive turns left from a cattle grid go over a stile on the right and enter a meadow, crossing this corner to corner (slightly right) in the direction of Lechlade's church steeple, which is partly obscured by trees. As you cross the meadow notice the fine old chestnut trees with their skewed trunks, also Lechlade Manor, in view to your right. The house is mid-19th century and now functions as a convent school.

A gate and footbridge link the meadow to a cricket field, and two more gates take the path finally to a road. Turning right at the road, you could follow this straight back to Lechlade's Market Place, but for an interesting alternative you could turn first left into Wharf Lane (which once led to a commercial wharf on the Thames) and return to the Market Place by way of the churchyard. From the churchyard path you will see the imposing Church House, with a gazebo set in the wall. The path is known as Shelley's Walk on account of a poem composed here in 1815. A wall plaque seen as you leave the path commemorates this literary event.